NIGEL RICHARDSON

KEY
Books

AIRLINES SERIES, VOLUME 12

Front cover image: Embraer E175 G-FBJA departing from Manchester Airport in June 2015. (Nigel Richardson)

Back cover image: Bombardier (de Havilland) Dash 8-Q402 G-JEDV at Manchester Airport in July 2015. (Nigel Richardson)

Title page image: Embraer E195 G-FBEJ, painted in a special 'Welcome to Yorkshire' livery. (Riik@mctr – Flickr, distributed under a Creative Commons CC BY-SA 2.0 Licence)

Contents page image: Bombardier (de Havilland) Dash 8-Q402 G-JECN at Manchester Airport. (Nigel Richardson)

Acknowledgements
I would like to thank the following photographers and organisations for kindly allowing the use of their images in the book: Fergus Bell, Don Bennett, Martin Bridges, Britten-Norman Aircraft Preservation Society (BNAPS), Rene Buschmann, Chris England, Derek Ferguson, Barry Friend, Lewis Grant, Danny Grew, Joop de Grot, Udo Haafke, David Hamilton, Gerard Helmer, Ian Howat, Rhys, Jones, LRS747, Neil McDonald, Tony Merton Jones, David Montgomery, Peter Moore, John Murdoch, Trent Nickson, David Oates, James Pearson, Neil Pidduck, Les Rickman, Dave Richardson, Ron Roberts, Fred Seggie, Paul Seymour, Kev Slade, John, Visanich, Maarten Visser and Fred Willemsen. I would also like to acknowledge and thank the following photographers for making available their work through Wikimedia Commons/Creative Commons: Aero Icarus, Aero Pixels, Pedro Aragao, Ardfern, Aldo Bidini, calflier001, Dale Coleman, Markus Eigenheer, James, Ken Fielding, Steve Fitzgerald, Flybyeigenjeer, Mike Freer, Felix Goetting, Rob Hodgkins, Steve Knight, Ronnie Macdonald, Torsten Maiwald, Eduard Marmet, Alan McKnight, MilborneOne, Paul Nelhams, Tim Rees, Riik@mctr, Bene Riobo, Ronnie Robertson, Paul Spijkers, Bjorn Strey, John Taggart, Rolf Wallner, Gary Watt, Konstantin von Wedelstaedt, Anna Zvereva. Finally, I would like to thank my wife, Gill, for carefully proofreading each chapter of the book.

Published by Key Books
An imprint of Key Publishing Ltd
PO Box 100
Stamford
Lincs PE9 1XQ

www.keypublishing.com

The right of Nigel Richardson to be identified as the author of this book has been asserted in accordance with the Copyright, Designs and Patents Act 1988 Sections 77 and 78.

Copyright © Nigel Richardson, 2023

ISBN 978 1 80282 357 8

Typeset by SJmagic DESIGN SERVICES, India.

Contents

Introduction

In 2007, Flybe was Europe's largest regional airline. By 2020 it had ceased operating, only to reappear two years later as Flybe 2.0.

Launched originally as Jersey European Airways from the merger of Intra Airways and Express Air Services in 1979, the airline operated passenger and cargo flights between the Channel Islands and mainland UK using mainly Douglas DC-3 Dakotas. After being bought out by the Walker Steel Group in 1983, Jersey European established its headquarters and maintenance facilities at Exeter Airport, which became an important hub for the airline.

Once Jersey European had gained a foothold at London Gatwick in 1993, British Aerospace 146 jets were introduced into the fleet. A franchise partnership with Air France followed and, by the turn of the century, Jersey European had developed an extensive route network within the UK and had also branched into Europe. With the Channel Islands then accounting for only a small proportion of the airline's business, Jersey European was renamed British European in 2000. Just two years later, the airline changed its name again to Flybe and repositioned itself as a low-fare airline; its aim was to be more competitive in the challenging global aviation environment, which had resulted from the 9/11 terrorist attacks in the USA. Interesting fleet changes followed with the acquisition of high-performance and fuel-efficient Bombardier Dash 8-Q400s, an aircraft that would become a mainstay of Flybe's operations, and the purchase of Embraer E195 turbofan airliners, a decision that would eventually contribute to the demise of the Flybe company.

When Flybe completed the acquisition of British Airways Connect in 2007, it effectively became the largest regional airline in Europe. A franchise agreement with Loganair followed and by the end of 2010 Flybe had an extensive route network served by a modern fleet of aircraft. The time seemed right to list the company on the London Stock Exchange, the airline being valued at £215 million. While the airline strived to expand in order to meet shareholder's expectations, it was faced with a growing number of challenges, including the state of the UK economy following the global financial crisis of 2007–08, the rising price of aviation fuel and the increase of Air Passenger Duty on UK domestic flights. Financial losses became an almost annual feature during the ten-year period subsequent to flotation on the Stock Exchange. Although restructuring, rebranding, improvement plans, fleet and route network rationalisation were all attempted, the recovery strategies all seemed to include an element of growth and expansion as a way out of the problem.

In 2019, Flybe was taken over by the Connect Airways Consortium, with shares in the airline valued at only 1p per share. The airline was rebranded as Virgin Connect, but continuing financial difficulties were compounded by the outbreak of the Covid-19 pandemic. A short-term rescue loan, sought from the UK government, was not forthcoming, despite a deal supposedly being agreed and Flybe went into administration in March 2020.

In April 2022, Flybe returned as an entirely new company, Flybe Ltd (formerly Thyme Opco, a company related to the US hedge fund firm Cyrus Capital). Using leased Bombardier Dash 8-Q400s, the 'new' Flybe introduced 23 routes during summer 2022, serving airports in the UK, France and the Netherlands.

Chapter 1
In the Beginning

The United Kingdom tourism industry started to expand after World War Two, with holidaymakers seeking relatively inexpensive holidays in locations providing sandy beaches, good weather and the same language and currency as at home. This resulted in a significant increase in the number of tourists from the UK visiting the two main Channel Islands of Jersey and Guernsey during the 1950s, which peaked in the late 1960s and early 1970s. The Channel Islands offered significant cost advantages to UK tourists. There was no purchase tax (replaced by VAT in 1973), which meant that many luxury items such as jewellery, cosmetics, perfumes, electrical goods, alcoholic drinks and tobacco products were all cheaper and in plentiful supply. Petrol prices were also lower and combined with cheap car hire and less expensive air and sea travel costs, compared favourably with other holiday destinations. Air travel was provided by both established and new start-up airlines, which were prepared to compete with sea-travel operators. One of the new operators in the growing and expanding leisure market was Intra Airways.

Intra Airways

Intra Airways was formed on the 1 January 1969, by a group that included several former British United Airways (C.I) pilots. Captains GL Gillborn and DH Stuart assumed the roles of Managing Director and Chief Pilot/Operations Manager respectively, as well as being Intra's first flight crew members. Based at Jersey Airport, the airline was initially established to operate inter-island air services in the Channel Islands. However, an efficient inter-island service in the Channel Islands had already been launched by Aurigny Air Services and they strongly contested the licence application from Intra to operate inter-island schedules. Therefore, for the first three years of its existence, Intra focused on passenger and cargo charters to locations further afield, using a single Douglas DC-3 Dakota aircraft (G-AKNB), which was fitted out with 36 passenger seats. One of the first charters was a cargo flight between Jersey and Bournemouth (Hurn) Airport on the 25 February 1969.

During the summer of 1969, Intra operated inclusive charter flights from Jersey and Guernsey to a number of locations in northwest France. Many flights involved carrying both day-trippers and holidaymakers between the Channel Islands and various parts of France and the UK mainland. Some freight charters were also undertaken, including daily newspaper flights from Gatwick Airport to Jersey and Guernsey on behalf of British United (C.I.) Airways. On 22 March 1970, Intra flew the first of many freight services transporting Channel Islands' flowers and vegetables between Jersey and Bournemouth. Flights to northwest France continued during 1970 and, in May 1970, Intra started a weekly inclusive tour charter service between Ostend and Jersey on behalf of a Belgian travel agent, carrying Belgian holidaymakers to the Channel Islands.

At the time of its formation, Intra Airways applied to the Air Transport Licensing Board (ATLB) for a licence to operate scheduled services between Jersey and Guernsey and the UK. The licence was finally granted in 1971, leading to Intra taking over the Gloucester (Staverton) to Jersey route from British Midland Airways. Intra acquired a second Dakota (G-AMPY) and leased several Britten-Norman BN-2A Islanders from Aurigny Air Services in order to handle the increased number of flights. Intra's first scheduled weekly service started at the beginning of April 1971, gradually increasing to six flights per week with the growing popularity of Jersey as a holiday destination and the demand for seats from tourists. A scheduled service between Guernsey and Staverton also started in 1971, and Intra formed Breakaway Holidays to specifically benefit from the Channel Islands-inclusive tour holiday market, using Intra Airways' services.

An additional UK scheduled service was added in May 1972, between Jersey and Cambridge, together with seasonal charter services from Jersey to Caen, northwest France and Brussels. A third Dakota (G-AMYJ) was added to the fleet in August 1972.

In November 1972, Intra acquired International Air Charter, a small Jersey-based air taxi company that operated a Piper PA-23 Aztec and a Piper Apache 235 aircraft on regular trips to the south of England and northern France. While covering the air taxi business, the smaller aircraft were often used during the winter months to cover Intra's scheduled routes when loads were small and didn't warrant the use of the larger Dakota aircraft.

Douglas DC-3 Dakota G-AKNB, the first aircraft to be used by Intra Airways. (Chris England)

The second Douglas DC-3 Dakota (G-AMPY) to be acquired by Intra Airway photographed in December 1970. (Rob Hodgkins, distributed under a Creative Commons CC BY-SA 2.0 Licence)

Douglas DC-3 Dakota G-AMYJ joined Intra in August 1972. (Mike Freer, distributed under a Creative Commons GNU FDL 1.2 Licence)

A significant milestone was achieved in December 1972 when Intra commenced its first all-freight scheduled service between Jersey and Bournemouth. Initially the route was shared with British Air Ferries (BAF), but in October 1973 BAF withdrew from the arrangement and it became entirely operated by Intra, with up to four Dakota flights per day, some flights routing to Jersey, others to Guernsey. The freight was predominantly flowers, fruit and vegetables during the spring and summer and a variety of cargo at other times of the year. The success of the service led to Bournemouth Airport establishing a dedicated cargo terminal with Intra as its main customer.

By the summer of 1973, Intra had four Dakotas in service, having acquired G-AMPZ in March of that year. Intra then extended its scheduled service network with the introduction of new routes linking Jersey with several locations in northern France (Deauville and Morlaix) and Ostend in Belgium. The introduction into service of two BN-2A Islanders (G-BAVT and G-BBZD) in 1974 coincided with the start of services from Deauville, Normandy to Gatwick Airport in April (although this was dropped in early 1975 due to limited demand), and Jersey to St. Brieuc in June. Despite the Civil Aviation Authority (CAA) approving Intra's application to operate a scheduled service between Jersey/Guernsey and Shoreham with up to 30 flights per week, the licence only covered a passenger service; Intra had planned to use Dakotas on these routes to carry both passengers and cargo.

In order to provide more capacity in response to the increasing number of routes and operations at various times during the summer of 1974, Intra chartered Dan-Air Hawker Siddeley 748s for the service between Jersey and Ostend, and Handley Page Dart Heralds belonging to British Island Airways for some flights from Jersey to Caen and Deauville.

February 1975 saw the injection of new capital into Intra from the Bernell Finance Group, which obtained a 55 percent stake in the airline. Three new board members were added, including Welsh businessman Bernard Haddican, owner of the Glamair air taxi company and Severn Airways. Haddican became the new Managing Director of Intra. The two Piper aircraft of International Air Charter were transferred to Glamair as part of the deal. Haddican soon bought out the Bernell Finance Group's interest in Intra to become the majority shareholder.

With the additional financial input from Haddican, Intra was able to purchase two more Dakotas (G-AMHJ; G-AMPO) from Humber Airways in mid-1975, and at the same time it sold its Islanders to become an all-Dakota operator again. One of the new Dakotas (G-AMHJ) was immediately moved to Scotland and based at Aberdeen where Intra began providing support to the oil business on behalf of Peters Aviation. G-AMHJ flew regular flights between Aberdeen and Sumburgh, Shetland, carrying

Douglas DC-3 Dakota G-AMPZ at Bournemouth (Hurn) Airport in September 1975. This aircraft was converted for freight-only use in 1977. (Steve Fitzgerald, distributed under a Creative Commons GNU FDL 1.2 Licence)

Britten-Norman BN-2A Islander G-BAVT was one of two Islanders acquired by Intra Airways and introduced into service in 1974. (Tony Merton Jones)

Britten-Norman BN-2A Islander G-BAVT at Jersey prior to introduction into service. (Ron Roberts Collection via Barry Friend)

Douglas DC-3 Dakota G-AMHJ was acquired by Intra from Humber Airways in May 1975 and was immediately based at Aberdeen to be used on operations in support of the oil industry. (Rob Hodgkins, distributed under a Creative Commons CC BY-SA 2.0 Licence)

oil-rig workers and equipment. The second newly acquired Dakota (G-AMPO) was also soon involved with oil-support charters. These activities indirectly led to a significant amount of ad hoc charter work for the airline to and from Scotland's airports, including Jersey to Glasgow, Benbecula to Blackpool and Brussels to Glasgow. The associated company, Breakaway Holidays, generated a significant amount of inclusive tour work from several regional airports in Scotland to the Channel Islands.

During the latter part of 1975, Intra began looking for more modern turbo-prop aircraft for use on its longer and busier routes, such as Jersey to Cambridge, Caen and Ostend. In March 1976, it leased a Vickers Viscount 700 Series aircraft (G-BDRC) from Alidair for 13 months. Over the next two years, as the Viscount fleet increased to four aircraft, the number of Dakotas was reduced such that only four of these aircraft were in operation.

Intra's operations through Staverton Airport, Gloucestershire, peaked during the summer of 1977, with Dakotas and a Viscount 700 operating a large number of weekend services to the Channel Islands. Intra's Breakaway Holidays generated a large amount of business through inclusive holiday tours and some other companies, including Marina Holidays, Gala Holidays, Jetline Holidays and Deeside Travel, were also using Intra Airways' services. The freight services between Jersey and Bournemouth remained successful and two Dakotas (G-AKNB and G-AMPZ) were converted to freighter-only use and almost entirely dedicated to this route. In January 1977, a Channel Island freight company, Express Air Freight, took over the operation of the two Dakotas, although they continued to be flown by Intra aircrew. Express Air Freight was associated with Air Bridge Carriers, based at East Midlands Airport; subsequently Intra, in association with Air Bridge Carriers, started a weekly freight service between Guernsey and East Midlands, followed by an East Midlands to Amsterdam route in October 1977 for British Midland.

Intra added two Vickers Viscount Series 800 aircraft to its fleet between the latter part of 1977 and the beginning of 1978 (G-BAPE and G-BAPG), the Series 700 aircraft, G-BDRC, having been returned to Alidair in October 1977. Intra's business was booming; the airline was gradually expanding its scheduled operations as well as continuing to operate a range of charter flights both on a regular and ad hoc basis. In 1978, Intra operated scheduled passenger flights from Jersey to Cambridge, Staverton and Swansea in the UK, Caen, Deauville, Dinard, Nantes and St. Brieuc in France, Ostend and Brussels in Belgium and Dusseldorf in Germany. Summer passenger charter flights included Gatwick to Dublin, Antwerp and Amsterdam using Vickers Viscounts, and day-trip flights from Gatwick to Amsterdam and Paris. In September 1978, a regular Sunday-only service was introduced between London Gatwick and Corunna in northern Spain. Intra's all-freight operations consisted of scheduled services between Jersey and Guernsey and between the Channel Islands and Bournemouth, and regular charter flights using Dakotas to transport newspapers from Luton Airport to Belfast Aldergrove Airport. The success of the Viscounts on many of the operations led to Intra beginning to run down its use of the Dakota on passenger flights. Two of the aircraft were sold to Eastern Airways in July 1978 (G-AMPO and G-AMRA), followed by a third in November 1978 (G-AMYJ).

By 1978, most of the airline's assets (90 percent) had been incorporated into Intra Holdings Ltd., including Exeter-based West Country Aircraft Servicing, which had been used by Intra to carry out most of the maintenance and servicing work on its aircraft. However, Intra's Managing Director, Bernard Haddican, was charged with allowing breaches of the Air Navigation Order by encouraging flight crews to exceed their permitted flying hours over a three-year period from January 1976 to

In March 1976, Intra Airways leased Vickers Viscount 700 Series G-BDRC from Alidair for use on its longer and busier routes. (Rob Hodgkins, distributed under a Creative Commons CC BY-SA 2.0 Licence)

Vickers Viscount 800 Series G-BAPG joined Intra in January 1978. (LRS747)

Vickers Viscount 800 Series G-BAPE at Coventry Airport in July 1978. (Rob Hodgkins, distributed under a Creative Commons CC BY-SA 2.0 Licence)

November 1978 and, on one occasion, of having allegedly flown a Viscount service himself without the appropriate commercial pilot's licence. Nearly 2,000 breaches of aviation law had been committed by Intra Airways over the same period. Haddican stepped down as Managing Director and, in January 1979, sold his holding to the Express Air Freight Group, which became a majority shareholder along with Jersey businessman John Habin, owner of the air charter company Aviation Beaufort.

Express Air Freight/Express Air Services

The origin of Express Air Services (EAS) is linked with two businesses by Art Carpenter in 1971: Carpenter's Air Services Ltd and Carpenters Transport Ltd. Carpenter's Air Services contracted space on cargo airlines to ship fresh flowers from Guernsey to the UK mainland. Initially, two Douglas Dakotas (G-AKNB and G-AMPZ) were chartered from Intra Airways, operating into Bournemouth and East Midlands Airports. Carpenter's Transport Ltd arranged for the distribution and delivery of the flowers to wholesale markets on the UK mainland. In 1975, the two businesses became part of a new company called Express Air Freight (CI) with Art Carpenter as Director. The respective roles of the two strands were retained but fell under the umbrella of one organisation. In January 1977, Express Air Freight, then owned by the Hutton group through Field Aviation, took over the operation of the two Dakotas it had been chartering from Intra Airways, and later purchased two Handley Page Dart Herald aircraft that were also operated by Intra on its behalf. Operations using the Heralds to fly flowers and fresh produce from the Channel Islands to Bournemouth Airport and consumer goods from the UK to the Channel Islands began in January 1978. The Guernsey to East Midlands Airport route was operated in association with Air Bridge Carriers, another subsidiary company of Field Aviation based at East Midlands Airport.

Two more Handley Page Dart Heralds were acquired in early 1978, which allowed the introduction of passenger charter flights under the title Express Air Services, with the first service being undertaken for Dan-Air on 17 March 1978 between Jersey and Bournemouth.

Express Air Freight (EAF) purchased two Handley Page HPR.7 Dart Herald Series 200s in August 1977, one of which, G-BEZB, is shown here. (LRS747)

Handley Page HPR.7 Dart Herald Series 200 G-ATDS was initially operated on freight flights by Intra Airways on behalf of Express Air Freight. In 1978 it began operating passenger services under the Express Air Services (EAS) title. (Eduard Marmet, distributed under a Creative Commons BY-SA 3.0 Licence)

Handley Page HPR.7 Dart Herald Series 200 G-BFRJ was acquired by Express Air Services in April 1978 to provide additional capacity for the introduction of passenger services. (Udo Haafke)

Chapter 2

The Early Years

Following the sale of Bernard Haddican's holding in Intra Airways to the Express Air Freight Group in January 1979, a major reorganisation resulted in the merger of the two organisations, which created the nucleus of Jersey European Airways. The other majority shareholder was John Habin, a Jersey resident, who owned Aviation Beaufort, an air charter/taxi business and Piper dealership. Habin intended Jersey European to establish several key routes from Jersey to major airports in the UK.

At the beginning of 1979, Intra had three Viscounts (G-AVJB, G-BAPE and G-BAPG) but its Dakota fleet had been reduced to just two aircraft (G-AMHJ and G-AMPY), with only one retaining the 36-seat passenger configuration. During the transition to Jersey European, Intra continued to use the Viscounts on summer-season scheduled flights and weekend charters linking the Channel Islands with Amsterdam, Brussels, Cambridge, Carlisle, Edinburgh, Newcastle, Ostend, Swansea and Bournemouth (the latter for Dan-Air). Services from Birmingham and Gatwick were also flown by the Viscounts, together with a significant number of ad-hoc charters to locations in Europe. However, the favoured Jersey to Staverton route lost popularity and was withdrawn in April 1979.

Jersey European Airways began trading on the 1 November 1979 under the chairmanship of John Habin. Under the new arrangements, some of Intra's scheduled routes were retained, including the Jersey–Cambridge passenger service, the Channel Islands–Bournemouth cargo link and a Royal Mail delivery contract between Bournemouth, Bristol and Liverpool, using the inherited Vickers Viscount, HP Herald and Dakota aircraft and operated under the Express Air Services banner. Shorter routes to nearby French coastal resorts in Normandy and Brittany and between the Channel Islands were operated by Jersey European using Piper PA-31 Navajos and Britten-Norman BN-2A Islanders and, later, Embraer EMB-110 Bandeirantes.

Vickers Viscount 814 G-AVJB, painted in the first Jersey European Airways livery following the formation of the airline in November 1979. (David A. Montgomery)

Vickers Viscount 814 G-AVJB was one of three Viscounts initially used by Jersey European and is shown here at East Midlands Airport in 1980. (Rene Buschmann Collection via Joop de Grot)

Significant changes to the fleet began in May 1980 with the introduction of a de-Havilland Canada DHC-6 Twin Otter, eventually building up to four of these aircraft. The route network was also refined, with new flights from the Channel Islands to Shoreham, Stansted, Paris and Brussels operating alongside the existing inter-island and French operations. On the 1 July 1980, Jersey European took over Haywards Aviation of Shoreham, which flew regular services to the Channel Islands and Dieppe out of Shoreham Airport.

In October 1980, Express Air Services withdrew from the partnership with Jersey European to resume operations under its own title. With it went the four HP Heralds; the Dakotas and Viscounts were sold. Express Air Services was renamed Channel Express in 1983, and the Dart Group PLC, to which the Channel Express Group belonged, established the Jet2.com brand in 2002.

Following the demerger of Express Air Services, Jersey European operated with a fleet of smaller, island-hopping, commuter aircraft during 1981 and 1982. These included two BN-2A Islanders, one of which left in September 1981, two EMB-110 Bandeirantes and four DHC-6 Twin Otters, three of which were leased from the British Antarctic Survey.

One of the first Britten-Norman BN-2A-26 Islanders, G-BESO, to be operated by Jersey European. (BNAPS Archive Collection)

Britten-Norman BN-2A-26 Islander G-AXXJ before joining Jersey European in March 1983. (Chris England)

Embraer EMB-110 Bandeirante G-BIBE at Dusseldorf in April 1987. (Danny Grew)

In 1981 Jersey European leased two de Havilland DHC-6-310 Twin Otters from the British Antarctic Survey. One of those aircraft, VP-FAQ is shown here at Southend Airport. (David Oates)

De Havilland DHC-6-310 Twin Otter G-BKBC at Jersey in June 1983. This aircraft was previously registered as VP-FAQ. (Eduard Marmet, distributed under a Creative Commons GNU FDL 1.2 Licence)

In November 1983, John Habin sold his entire capital share of Jersey European to the Walker Steel Group from Blackburn, Lancashire, owned by entrepreneur and businessman Jack Walker. The Walker Steel Group was already involved in commercial aviation as owners of Spacegrand Aviation, a Blackpool-based charter airline established in 1979 as an air-taxi and executive commuter service company operating out of Blackpool Airport. Following a failed attempt at a merger with Air UK, Spacegrand began scheduled services to Belfast and Dublin from Blackpool in August 1981 using a Piper PA-23 Aztec. In 1982, the Isle of Man was included in Spacegrand's scheduled operations and two Piper PA-31 Navajo Chieftains were added to the fleet. Spacegrand played a key role in the opening up of Short Brothers Belfast Harbour airfield (which became Belfast City Airport) to scheduled airline services. With passenger demand beginning to exceed the capacity provided by the three Pipers, Spacegrand introduced three DHC-6 Twin Otter 300s to the fleet between September 1982 and March 1983. At this stage, the company was looking for opportunities to develop and expand its aviation business interests. Jersey European had a similar fleet and operation, as well as an aircraft maintenance facility (JEA (Engineering) Ltd), which could also be used for Spacegrand's aircraft. Investment by the Walker Steel Group offered a very good base from which to develop.

Initially, Jersey European and Spacegrand operated as two largely separate entities; each retained its characteristic brand despite partially shared management, although some cross-sharing of Twin Otter aircraft took place. Exeter Airport acted as the hub linking the two route networks. In the latter part of 1983 and early 1984, Jersey European took the first steps to develop and modernise its fleet by adding a

Short SD330 aircraft were introduced into the Jersey European fleet in early 1984 as part of fleet modernisation. Shown here is G-BJUK at Jersey Airport in July 1987. (Peter Moore)

Short SD330 G-BJFK at Exeter Airport. (Neil Pidduck)

Short SD360 G-OJSY was the first aircraft of the type to be added to the Jersey European fleet in March 1986. (Rob Hodgkins, distributed under a Creative Commons CC BY-SA 2.0 Licence)

Short SD360 G-OBOH on final approach to Guernsey Airport in August 1988. (Udo Haafke, distributed under a Creative Commons GNU FDL 1.2 Licence)

Fokker F27-100 Friendship and a Short SD330 aircraft. Towards the end of the 1980s, F27 Friendships and the Short SD360 aircraft became standard components of the Jersey European fleet. Jersey European began to fly services between Gatwick, Bristol and Cardiff in the summer of 1984, on behalf of British Caledonian Commuter, taking over services from Genair.

In April 1985, Spacegrand leased a Short SD330 from the manufacturer, which allowed the establishment of new routes between Bristol, Cardiff and Teeside. Finally, on the 26 October 1985, Jersey European and Spacegrand became fully amalgamated as a subsidiary of Walker Aviation, with Jersey European Airways becoming the surviving title. Spacegrand's three Twin Otter aircraft and its programme of scheduled flights linking Blackpool, Birmingham, Teeside, Belfast, Dublin and the Isle of Man were all eventually integrated into the combined operator, and the headquarters of Jersey European was established at Exeter. The annual turnover of Jersey European was reported as just under £9m in 1985, during which the airline carried 160,000 passengers and employed 135 staff.

In order to diversify the business, the activities of Walker Aviation's subsidiary, Guide Aviation Leasing, were significantly enlarged in co-operation with Alexander Aviation/Euroair, Business Air and later, BAC Express. Alongside the established scheduled flights, Jersey European operated general charters and a Royal Mail contract at night between Exeter and Liverpool using an EMB-110 Bandeirante. At the beginning of 1986, Jersey European gave up its routes from Shoreham to South East Air, and returned one of its Twin Otter aircraft to the lessor.

Although it had been Jersey European's intention to grow its fleet of pressurised Fokker F27 aircraft from the two acquired in 1988, there was a shortage of the newer and larger F27-500 variant, which was capable of carrying 48 passengers in a four-abreast configuration, that the airline wanted for use on its higher-density routes. As a short-term solution, three Hawker Siddeley 748 aircraft were leased in mid–late 1989 to cover some Channel Islands, Dublin and Belfast services, as well as a new Royal Mail Datapost contract. Two of the 748s remained with Jersey European to the end of 1991, and one was held on fleet until July 1992. The situation concerning the availability of F27 aircraft improved in 1990 and five former Australian aircraft were acquired at various stages towards the end of the year, with another one in January 1991.

In 1989, JEA (Engineering) Ltd, originally formed as a separate company on Jersey in 1980 for the servicing and maintenance of Jersey European's aircraft, moved to Exeter. It took over a company that had previously been used by Intra Airways for aircraft maintenance, West Country Aviation Services, and its hangar facilities at the airport. The resulting aircraft engineering and servicing base was renamed Jersey European Technical Services. It became a CAA-approved facility in 1990 and was able to handle up to 40 commercial aircraft up to Fokker F27 size, employing 180 staff by 1991.

One of the three Hawker Siddeley 748s (G-BGMN) leased by Jersey European at the end of the 1980s to provide increased capacity on its higher density routes. (Lewis Grant)

Hawker Siddeley 748 G-BGMO at Southampton Airport in April 1990. This aircraft was acquired by Jersey European in October 1989. (Paul Seymour)

Fokker F27-500 G-JEAB went into service with Jersey European in April 1988 and provided seating for 48 passengers in a four-abreast seating configuration. (Udo Haafke, distributed under a Creative Commons GNU FDL 1.2 Licence)

Approaching Gatwick Airport, in May 1991, is Fokker F27-500 G-JEAA. The aircraft is painted in the new Jersey European livery. (Tim Rees, distributed under a Creative Commons GNU FDL 1.2 Licence)

By 1990, Jersey European had established a substantial route network, which was separated into two distinct geographical areas, partly as a result of the previous activities of the two strands that made up the airline. The northern and southern route networks were inter-linked by flights through Birmingham, Bristol and Exeter. The success of the route network was reflected in passenger numbers, which had grown to 460,000 in 1990, an increase of 40 percent on the previous year. Further development of the route network was facilitated by the demise of Air Europe and Dan-Air in the early 1990s due to financial difficulties. The opportunity arose for Jersey European to establish itself at London Gatwick by taking up vacated routes to Jersey, Guernsey and Belfast, thus linking Belfast with the Channel Islands. This was a major breakthrough for the airline. From 1992, Leeds/Bradford was added to the number of regional airports available from Belfast City Airport, followed by Birmingham in 1993, via which an additional link to the Channel Islands from Northern Ireland was available. The original Exeter hub was now complemented by connections at London and Birmingham.

A significant upgrade of Jersey European's fleet occurred in 1993 when the airline received its first jet aircraft, a British Aerospace 146. The BAe 146 is a short-haul, regional airliner. Despite having four engines, it is efficient and very quiet to operate and, as a consequence, was marketed under the name 'Whisperjet'. The short take off and landing performance of the airliner made it ideally suited for operating out of the small regional airports served by Jersey European. Initially two BAe 146-200 Series and one larger 146-300 Series aircraft were acquired in March 1993 for use on flights originating from

Left: Jersey European received its first jet aircraft, the British Aerospace 146, in 1993. BAe 146-200 G-JEAJ was one of the first aircraft to be delivered, initially registered as G-OLCA. (Ardfern, distributed under a Creative Commons GNU FDL 1.2 Licence)

Below: Another BAe146-200, G-JEAK, at Galileo Galilei Airport, Pisa, Italy in June 1995. (Aldo Bidini, distributed under a Creative Commons GNU FDL 1.2 Licence)

Above: BAe 146-300 G-JEAM at Gatwick Airport in 1994. The fuselage of the 146-300 is stretched by 3.2m compared with the -200 variant. (LRS747)

Right: Arriving at Luton Airport in June 1999 is BAe146-300 G-JEBE. (Torsten Maiwald, distributed under a Creative Commons GNU FDL 1.2 Licence)

Gatwick, with the aircraft based at Belfast City, Gatwick and Jersey Airports. An additional BAe 146-300 Series aircraft followed in May for operations between Birmingham and Belfast. The introduction of the BAe 146 freed up most of the eight Fokker F27 aircraft in the fleet to cover increasing frequencies of flights on other routes, and for flying ad hoc charters, especially weekend flights to the Channel Islands, as well as for acting as standby aircraft.

A number of Jersey European's services focused on the business traveller, with several daily rotations to meet their needs. Following the arrival of the BAe 146 into the fleet, a Business Class service was introduced on some aircraft. This included in-flight leather seats, preferential seat selection and separate check-in areas at airports. Jersey European was the first UK airline to offer two classes of service on its domestic flights at that time. In addition, separate lounges for business travellers were opened at Belfast City, Jersey and Guernsey airports.

In an attempt to foster and reward passenger loyalty, a frequent-flyer programme called 'Ticket to Freedom' was introduced. The high service standard provided by the airline was greatly appreciated by the growing number of passengers and the travel industry as a whole. It was reflected in the award of 'Best UK Regional Airline' by the Northern Ireland Travel and Tourism Board in 1993 and 1994.

Although Jersey European had incurred losses of £3.7 million during the 1993–94 financial year, which led to a reduction in the size of its workforce, the number of BAe 146 aircraft in the fleet continued to slowly increase as the domestic route network expanded the following year. It included the introduction of services from London Stansted to Belfast City and the integration of Belfast International Airport into the network, supplementing flights from Belfast City Airport. A Belfast to Luton service was also trialled for a short period of time. Continental Europe was also added into the route network; operations between London Stansted and Marseille in southern France began on behalf of Air Inter, and Belfast to Amsterdam through a code-sharing arrangement with Air UK. The expansion proved successful with pre-tax profits of £1.8 million in 1995.

In 1996, Jersey European entered a franchise partnership with Air France, which involved operating routes on Air France's behalf from London Heathrow Airport to Lyon and Toulouse, Jersey to Lyon and the take-over of Air France's Birmingham to Paris Charles de Gaulle Airport route. Three more BAe 146 aircraft were acquired for these routes, taking the total of BAe 146s in the fleet to ten, with a mixture of -100, -200 and -300 series variants. A number of the BAe 146 aircraft were painted in the Air France livery and Jersey European air crew wore the Air France uniform. The overall commercial responsibility for the venture, whether it led to a profit or loss, lay with Jersey European. Further development of the franchise followed with the introduction of services from Glasgow and Edinburgh to Paris.

The remainder of the fleet, in 1996, consisted of six Fokker F27 and two Short SD360 aircraft. All these aircraft were extensively refurbished in late 1996, aligning them with the airline's 'Regional Direct' economy class service standard, which included leather seats.

In 1997, Jersey European leased a BAC One-Eleven from European Aviation Air Charter for 20 months to operate the London Stansted to Belfast route and to fly some Air France schedules at times of aircraft shortage due to servicing and maintenance. Other new routes introduced that year included a daily flight from Bristol to the Isle of Man, flying an F27, and twice daily services to Exeter and the Channel Islands from Glasgow, using Birmingham as the connecting hub.

Fleet expansion continued in 1998 with the acquisition of five ex-Thai Airways BAe 146-300 aircraft, resulting in a total of 17 BAe 146 aircraft. The additional capacity allowed Jersey European to take over a daily Bristol (Filton) to Toulouse contract from Air Bristol for British Aerospace and to begin a three-times daily operation between Luton and Belfast from the 1 August 1998. Figures for the financial year 1998–99 showed that Jersey European had carried more than two million passengers with more than

On final approach to London Heathrow is BAe 146-100 G-JEAT, one of the first aircraft to be operated for Air France by Jersey European. (LRS747)

BAe 146-200 G-JEAS taxiing at London Heathrow in August 1999, operating for Air France as part of the franchise partnership with Jersey European. (Ken Fielding, distributed under a Creative Commons BY-SA 3.0 Licence)

Jersey European also operated the larger BAe146-300 for Air France, as seen here with G-JEBA. (Konstantin von Wedelstaedt, distributed under a Creative Commons GNU FDL 1.2 Licence)

BAC 1-11 510ED G-AVMK at Stansted Airport in June 1998. Jersey European leased this aircraft from European Aviation Air Charter for 20 months from March 1997. (Torsten Maiwald, distributed under a Creative Commons GNU FDL 1.2 Licence)

1,000 weekly flights serving 18 UK and six international destinations, which contributed to an annual turnover of almost £153 million.

A plan to float the company on the London Stock Exchange in November 1998, partly to fund investment in new aircraft, had to be abandoned when the market for aviation stock collapsed. The airline had expected to be valued at £100 million.

The need for Jersey European to replace its ageing turboprop fleet of five Fokker F27s and two Short SD360 aircraft gained impetus in 1999. It resulted in an £160 million order for 11 Bombardier (de-Havilland Canada) Dash 8-Q200, –Q300 and -Q400 variants and four Canadair (Bombardier) CRJ200 aircraft. The initial five Dash 8-Q311 aircraft arrived on lease from Bombardier between June and November 1999, the first of which operated the Southampton to Guernsey route in October 1999. The first of the four Canadair CRJ200s was delivered in October 1999, with two more arriving in 2000 and the final aircraft of the order delivered in January 2001. Two of the CRJ200s were operated sporting the Air France livery, predominantly on the Birmingham to Paris route.

As the new aircraft arrived, disposal of the Fokker F27-500s was taking place, with four aircraft departing between August and December 1999. The final UK scheduled passenger flight operated by a Jersey European F27-500 was on the 7 December 1999 when G-JEAH flew from Belfast City to

At the end of the 20th century, Jersey European began to replace the ageing turboprops in its fleet. One of the new acquisitions was the Bombardier (de Havilland) Dash 8-Q311, such as G-JEDD, seen here at Guernsey Airport. (Ian Howat)

Bombardier (de Havilland) Dash 8-Q311 G-JEDE at Birmingham Airport. (Paul Nelhams, distributed under a Creative Commons CC BY-SA 2.0 Licence)

Exeter. The last remaining F27 left the fleet in April 2000. One Short SD360 (G-OBHD) remained with the airline until November 2001 to operate the Exeter to Birmingham service, which generally had low passenger numbers, the Short SD360 being able to carry up to nine passengers. The route was eventually withdrawn due to low loads.

Towards the end of 1999, Jersey European entered into a code-share agreement with the Irish regional airline CityJet. The arrangement covered the Dublin to London City route that was being operated by CityJet and led to some cross-transfers of aircraft. CityJet went on to operate a Dublin–Jersey service on behalf of Jersey European's successor, British European, during the summer of 2000 using a BAe 146-100 (EI-CPY).

Jersey European now had a foothold at London City Airport and, in December 1999, launched a London City to Edinburgh service. At the time it was the only airline to have a presence at all four London airports, if only temporarily. The ability of the newly acquired Dash 8 aircraft over regional jets to more readily operate from shorter runways, such as the one at London City Airport, opened up opportunities for Jersey European to continue to develop its route network. New services were introduced from London City to Belfast, Aberdeen, the Isle of Man, Jersey and Leeds/Bradford Airport, although the Dublin and Leeds/Bradford routes were later withdrawn due to poor passenger uptake.

As the 1990s drew to a close, Jersey European had made significant inroads into modernising and growing its fleet of aircraft and had developed a fairly extensive route network concentrated on services from Exeter, Belfast, the London airports and Jersey/Guernsey, with Birmingham emerging as a major interconnecting hub.

Right: Britten-Norman BN-2A-26 Islander G-BESO at Jersey Airport. (BNAPS Archive Collection)

Below: Embraer EMB-110 Bandeirante G-BGYV operated for Jersey European from October 1985 to February 1988. (Rob Hodgkins, distributed under a Creative Commons CC BY-SA 2.0 Licence)

A Spacegrand Aviation de Havilland DHC-6-310 Twin Otter (G-BGMD) at Coventry Airport. Spacegrand Aviation was owned by the Walker Steel Group, which took over Jersey European in November 1983. The two airlines eventually amalgamated as a single entity. (Rob Hodgkins, distributed under a Creative Commons CC BY-SA 2.0 Licence)

Above: De Havilland DHC-6-310 Twin Otter G-BFGP of Spacegrand Aviation at Biggin Hill Airport in May 1984. (Steve Knight, distributed under a Creative Commons CC BY 2.0 Licence)

Left: Fokker F27-200 G-BAUR, which operated for Jersey European for eight months in 1995, approaching London Gatwick in June 1995. (Torsten Maiwald, distributed under a Creative Commons GNU FDL 1.2 Licence)

Fokker F27-500 G-JEAD at Manchester in 1995. (Ken Fielding, distributed under a Creative Commons BY-SA 3.0 Licence)

On final approach into London Gatwick is Fokker F27-500 G-JEAB. (Torsten Maiwald, distributed under a Creative Commons GNU FDL 1.2 Licence)

Short SD330 G-BJFK was acquired by Jersey European in April 1985 and remained with the airline for two and a half years. (Lewis Grant)

Short SD360 G-OBOH at Jersey Airport in June 1994. (Rolf Wallner, distributed under a Creative Commons GNU FDL 1.2 Licence)

The Short SD360, which could carry up to 39 passengers in a high-density seating configuration. G-BLZT, shown here, joined Jersey European in March 1992. (Alan McKnight, distributed under a Creative Commons GNU FDL 1.2 Licence)

Hawker Siddeley 748 G-BMFT at Dinard Airport, Saint-Malo, France. (Maarten Visser)

BAe 146-200 G-JEAK on final approach to London Gatwick in October 1993. (Torsten Maiwald, distributed under a Creative Commons GNU FDL 1.2 Licence)

From 1996, Jersey European began operating flights from London Heathrow to Toulouse and Lyon, Jersey to Lyon and Birmingham to Paris CDG on Air France's behalf. BAe 146-100 G-JEAU is in Air France livery. (Lewis Grant)

BAe146-100 G-JEAO was one of three BAe 146-100s operated for Air France by Jersey European. (LRS747)

Although in Air France livery, BAe146-300 G-JEBB is shown at Manchester in April 2000 operating a Jersey European service. (Ken Fielding, distributed under a Creative Commons BY-SA 3.0 Licence)

Bombardier (de Havilland) Dash 8-Q201 G-JEDY was acquired by Jersey European in March 2000, just before the airline changed its name to British European. (David J. Hamilton)

Chapter 3

Changing Names, Changing Focus

By the beginning of the 21st century, Jersey European was regarded as the UK's third largest airline and its biggest surviving independent airline. For a company that had once operated predominantly from the Channel Islands, it now had a significant presence in Northern Ireland and Scotland and was operating flights into mainland Europe for Air France. The name 'Jersey European' no longer seemed appropriate so, in May 2000, the airline changed its name to British European to reflect better its business markets and the routes being covered. In order to recognise and acknowledge the airline's recent heritage, the phrase 'a part of Walker Aviation' was added to the company's title.

Subsequent to the change of name, British European began to consider its future fleet and options for upgrading. In October 2001, it received its first, larger Bombardier Dash 8-Q400 Series aircraft, which resulted in the departure of its last remaining Short SD360 and the closure of services between Exeter and Birmingham. The four Canadair CRJ200 aircraft were not well suited to the airline's business requirements and route network, especially when operating from airports with short runways, and needed replacing. The performance characteristics and efficiency of the BAe 146, however, continued to be optimal for the operations of the regional carrier and the aircraft remained very popular with both passengers and aircrew.

In March 2001, British European signed a Memorandum of Understanding with BAe Systems for the firm order of 12 Avro RJX-100 airliners and a further eight options, and British European was to be the launch customer of the new airliner variant. The Avro RJX Series of aircraft represented an advanced upgrade of the BAe 146/Avro RJ Series, with new engines (Honeywell AS977 turbofans) for greater efficiency (15 percent less fuel burn), an improved and quieter performance (17 percent increased range) and a 20 percent reduction in maintenance costs. The deal was worth a reported £600 million and deliveries of the new aircraft were planned to take place from April 2002. Unfortunately, after building and test flying two prototypes and a production aircraft destined for British European, BAe Systems terminated the programme in December 2001 as a consequence of the 9/11 terrorists attacks against the USA and their impact on the aviation industry. Instead, BAe Systems offered to build 14 hybrid aircraft, but British European were not prepared to accept the risks associated with operating what essentially would be a unique type and declined the offer as a poor long-term option. The impact forced British European to delay its upgrading programme for another three years, during which the airline experienced major challenges.

After only three months in existence as British European, the owner Jack Walker died in August 2000. He had played a major role in overseeing the development of the airline since the takeover by the Walker Steel Group in 1983. One year later, British European was facing the effects of the post-9/11 downturn in the global aviation industry and, along with many other airlines, a substantial financial loss. The only airlines that seemed to be thriving in terms of growing networks and maintaining load factors (meaning the percentage of available seating capacity filled with passengers) were the low-cost airlines such as Ryanair and easyJet. British European were now facing the potential challenge of being squeezed out of the market, both by traditional airlines, such as British Airways and its UK partner airlines, and by low-cost operators. Under the guidance of the Chief Executive and Managing Director, Jim French, who was aware of the competitive nature of the regional and low-cost airline business from his experiences with Caledonian Airways and Air UK, a decision was taken to reposition British European in the low-fare sector. However, the airline was to retain its commitment to business travellers, its regional status and, most importantly, its excellent customer service and values. It was considered that a distinctive niche could be found by blending low fares with the high standard of service of traditional airlines, which it possessed already, such that the airline would not be regarded as low cost. The low-fare business model focused on reducing costs by charging passengers for in-flight catering, ticket-pricing similar to other low-cost airlines, a no-refund policy on tickets, a substantial increase in excess baggage charges and a significant shift to online ticket sales with a consequent reduction in distribution costs. The transformation came to fruition on the 18 July 2002, when British European was rebranded as Flybe.

The first Canadair (Bombardier) CRJ200 was delivered to Jersey European in October 1999. CRJ200 G-JECB, seen at Paris CDG Airport in August 2001, entered into service with British European in June 2000. (Aero Icarus, distributed under a Creative Commons BY-SA 2.0 Licence)

The third Canadair (Bombardier) CRJ200 G-JECC to be delivered to British European. The British European livery is slightly modified from that of Jersey European, with the order of the five bands of colour on the arrow logo reversed and the point of the arrow rotated by 45 degrees. (Danny Grew)

BAe 146-200 G-JEAV in British European livery at Paris CDG Airport in August 2001. (Aero Icarus, distributed under a Creative Commons BY-SA 2.0 Licence)

The longer BAe 146-300 G-JEBD at Manchester Airport in May 2001. (Ken Fielding, distributed under a Creative Commons BY-SA 3.0 Licence)

Bombardier (de Havilland) Dash 8-Q201 G-JEDZ went into service with British European just after the change of name in May 2000. (Gary Watt, distributed under a Creative Commons GNU FDL 1.2 Licence)

The Bombardier (de Havilland) Dash 8-Q311 has an airframe 3.43m longer than the -Q201 variant. DHC-8-Q311 G-JEDD at Bournemouth Airport. (Les Rickman, distributed under a Creative Commons GNU FDL 1.2 Licence)

Bombardier (de Havilland) Dash 8-Q402 G-JEDI was the first -Q400 variant acquired by British European in October 2001. (David Oates)

Initially Flybe offered Business, Premium Economy and 'no frills' Economy tickets. All tickets were available for booking online, which proved fortuitous; within six weeks of operating as Flybe, 40 percent of all bookings were made online compared with six percent in November 2001. In addition, there was an overall increase in bookings with 21 percent more passengers in the six-month period to October 2002 than in the equivalent period the previous year. The frequent-flyer reward scheme was renamed 'Passport to Freedom'. Flybe also introduced a Passenger Charter, which articulated clearly its service standards and guarantees, unlike other budget airlines. The Passenger Charter was displayed at every airport out of which Flybe operated, as well as on the company's website, and it outlined exactly what customers could expect of the airline and how Flybe would care for customers should things go wrong, such as compensation for flight delays or delayed baggage. In 2002, Jim French explained the philosophy behind the Passenger Charter, stating, 'We are a low-fares airline, yet we are dedicated to service. Customers should not have to sacrifice service for a low fare. With us they get both.'

Code share agreements, initially with Continental Airlines and later with Delta Airlines, were another significant development for Flybe in 2002. These gave Flybe the potential to offer flights to Newark (for New York) from Gatwick, Manchester, Birmingham, Belfast City, Guernsey, Jersey, Glasgow and Edinburgh, all with a Flybe (BE) flight number.

Although the effects of the 9/11 attacks led to a loss of £17 million in annual revenue for Flybe, and in spite of ongoing economic uncertainties, the airline pushed ahead with its network expansion. In 2003, it invested in a new hub at Southampton Airport. The decision was based on the absence of a low-fare airline serving the central southern region of the UK, which had a large catchment area encompassing the south coast, southwest, Thames Valley and South West London. Plans involved basing an initial four aircraft and the required air crew at Southampton, which could be increased to ten aircraft as the route network developed. Operations began in March with scheduled daily services to Milan Bergamo and Geneva and twice-daily services to Dublin, Belfast City, Guernsey and Jersey. Soon after, six new destinations for the summer months were added, including Murcia, Malaga, Toulouse, Alicante, Bergerac and Ibiza, followed by Barcelona and Nice for the winter schedules.

Increasing development of the route network resulted in Bristol Airport becoming a major centre for Flybe operations, starting with flights to Toulouse from October 2003, followed by Bordeaux, Bergerac and Jersey in 2004. The location of Flybe's headquarters and aircraft maintenance/servicing facility at Exeter led to that being the next airport to experience major expansion in 2004, with the addition of new routes to Alicante, Belfast City, Edinburgh, Glasgow, Malaga and Faro alongside its existing provision to Dublin, Jersey and Guernsey. Expansion of Liverpool John Lennon Airport followed in 2005, beginning with flights to Belfast City in February 2005 and flights to Glasgow, Edinburgh and Jersey, with the potential for further expansion during the summer months.

Flybe's franchise partnership with Air France came to an end in 2004. It has been suggested that Air France did not want a low-fare airline operating its services. The loss of the Air France business enabled Flybe to sell its valuable slots at London Heathrow, leading to a windfall of £17 million and making a significant contribution to the year-end profits reported in April 2004.

For some time, Flybe had been seeking to rationalise its aircraft fleet. Management felt that, in order for Flybe to exist as a new and effective airline in the low-fare sector, it would have to reduce the cost issues associated with a multi-type fleet and focus on using the most efficient types of aircraft on its route network. In 2003, the Flybe fleet comprised three different variants of the BAe 146 (the -100, -200 and -300 Series), four Canadair CRJ200s and Bombardier Dash 8-Q200, -Q300 and -Q400 aircraft. This variety of aircraft presented a host of operational and engineering problems and was not cost effective. The aim was to standardise the fleet into just two aircraft types: the BAe 146-300 and the Bombardier Dash 8-Q400. In April 2003, Flybe ordered 17 Dash 8-Q400 series aircraft with an option for a further 20; the first aircraft was to be delivered in June 2003 with the remainder over the following three years. These aircraft would eventually replace the smaller Dash 8-Q200 and -Q300 Series aircraft,

Rebranding and a name change to Flybe occurred in July 2002. This view of BAe 146-200 G-JEAW, taken shortly after take-off from Manchester Airport, displays the new Flybe livery. (Dale Coleman, distributed under a Creative Commons GNU FDL 1.2 Licence)

BAe 146-300 G-JEBD at Manchester Airport. The initial Flybe colour scheme included the name British European on the front fuselage and a band made up of four of the colours that featured in the Jersey European and British European arrow logo. (Aldo Bidini, distributed under a Creative Commons GNU FDL 1.2 Licence)

Bombardier (de Havilland) Dash 8-Q402 G-JEDU about to land at Birmingham Airport. This aircraft features the revised Flybe livery with the British European label and colour band on the front fuselage now replaced with six dots or lozenges of yellow, red and purple, now the main colours of the Flybe brand. (Rob Hodgkins, distributed under a Creative Commons CC BY-SA 2.0 Licence)

Bombardier (de Havilland) Dash 8-Q402 G-JECM at Manchester Airport. (Nigel Richardson)

and take over routes from the CRJ200s, which were to be discarded. The Bombardier Dash 8-Q400 was chosen owing to its high-speed performance, low-operating costs (the lowest seat cost on the market at the time), fast-turnaround capability, which allowed for up to ten flights to be flown daily, and low noise qualities, both in the cabin and externally. Although the Dash 8-Q400 had a relatively slower cruising speed compared to jet aircraft, such as the Boeing 737, this was compensated for by its fast climb rate, especially on sectors of less than 90 minutes. The aircraft could also be used economically on longer sectors. The four CRJ200 aircraft were sold to Air Sahara, India in July 2003, almost two years later than Flybe intended due to the cancellation of the Avro RJX order.

Following the addition of 16 new routes from its regional bases at Belfast City, Bristol, Exeter and Southampton in 2004, the summer of 2005 saw another 31 new routes being introduced. The summer timetable included the addition of both Leeds/Bradford and Norwich Airport to the airline's existing regional bases, with the major route expansions occurring at Southampton, Liverpool, Exeter and Birmingham. In total, 14 new routes were launched in Flybe's winter schedule for 2005/2006; Norwich International Airport gained six of these routes bringing the total number of routes, operated from the airport to ten. New routes from Birmingham and Southampton to Berne augmented its existing popular winter season ski routes to Chambéry, Geneva and Salzburg.

In July 2003, Flybe announced that it planned to start talks the following year over the potential sale or part-sale of the business. A number of parties were believed to be interested in purchasing the airline, which was valued at £100 million. The aim of a potential sale was to raise new capital to fund a £400 million programme to replace Flybe's BAe 146 aircraft with larger Boeing 737 or Airbus A320 family aircraft. Despite no sale materialising, Flybe made an announcement in June 2005 that it was to purchase up to 26 Embraer E195 aircraft (14 firm orders and 12 options) and be the launch customer of the Embraer E175/195 family, with the first delivery scheduled for September 2006. The Embraer E195 is a narrow-body, medium-range twin-turbofan airliner, which accommodates 112–124 passengers in a four-abreast seating configuration. Flybe had opted for the 118-seat regional airliner over 150-seat Airbus and Boeing aircraft due to its operational and cost advantages and outstanding environmental performance. The quiet General Electric CF34 turbofan engines are equipped with a digital engine control management system that continuously optimises the engine performance. The resulting advantages of reduced fuel consumption and maintenance requirements produces lower operating costs, and the noise reduction is particularly advantageous for operations into smaller, regional airports where noise restrictions are strict, such as London City Airport.

Flybe confirmed that the decision to replace the BAe 146 with the Embraer E195 completed the fleet rationalisation strategy begun in 2003, and it was hoped that the resulting fleet of young aircraft

Flybe wet-leased four Boeing 737-300s from Astraeus between May 2005 and December 2006, prior to the delivery of the Embraer E195. Pictured here is G-STRB at Manchester in July 2005. (Dale Coleman, distributed under a Creative Commons GNU FDL 1.2 Licence)

Boeing 737-300 G-STRI at Faro in September 2005. (Pedro Aragao, distributed under a Creative Commons CC BY-SA 3.0 Licence)

Embraer E195 G-FBEA was the first aircraft of the type to be delivered to Flybe in September 2006. (Pedro Aragao, distributed under a Creative Commons CC BY-SA 3.0 Licence)

Flybe acquired 14 Embraer E195 aircraft between September 2006 and October 2008. The second aircraft to be delivered was G-FBEB, shown here departing Birmingham Airport. (Rob Hodgkins, distributed under a Creative Commons CC BY-SA 2.0 Licence)

would provide a ten-year platform for profitable growth. In the interim, until delivery of the E195s was underway, Flybe wet-leased a number of Boeing 737-300 aircraft from Astraeus from mid-2005 through to December 2006. At any one time it had at least three Boeing 737s operating in the fleet. These aircraft enabled the start of new routes from Birmingham to Spain and Portugal, and similar longer sectors with high payloads from Exeter and Norwich. Delivery of the first two Embraer E195s took place in September and December 2006.

In January 2006, Manchester Airport was launched as Flybe's latest regional base, initially with two new routes to Belfast City and Exeter. By September, Flybe was serving 45 airports in nine European countries with more than 125 routes and a fleet of 39 aircraft. The switch to a low-fare business model had slowly achieved profitability despite a number of unforeseen challenges along the way. In the financial year up to March 2001, the airline lost £10.7 million, followed by a loss of almost £17 million in 2001/02 as a result of a downturn in trade due to the impact of the 9/11 attacks and foot-and-mouth travel restrictions. Operating losses more than doubled from £4.2 million in 2002/03 to £9.8 million in 2003/04 but the company was able to report a pre-tax profit of £2.9 million (up from £302,000 in 2002/03) due to a £17 million windfall from the sale of take-off and landing slots at London Heathrow after the end of the franchising deal with Air France. Profits increased to £6 million for the year ending 31 March 2006.

A significant contribution to both British European's and Flybe's profitability was the airline's aircraft maintenance and servicing subsidiary, Flybe Aviation Services (formerly British European Aviation Services), based at Exeter Airport. By 2001, this business was able to support more than 100 aircraft. A significant amount (up to 50 percent) of the work undertaken was third-party, predominantly for European airlines involving the maintenance of BAe 146, Bombardier CRJ and Dash 8, ATR 42 and ATR 72 and Short SD360 aircraft.

Right: Canadair (Bombardier) CRJ200 G-JECB on final approach to Brussels Airport in March 2002. (Paul Spijkers, distributed under a Creative Commons GNU FDL 1.2 Licence)

Below: Canadair (Bombardier) CRJ200 G-JECD at Glasgow International in February 2003. This aircraft and CRJ200 G-JECA were operated for Air France as part of the franchise partnership. (Fred Seggie)

Above: BAe146-300 G-JEAM at Manchester Airport in April 2003. The aircraft is painted in the British European livery despite the name change to Flybe in July 2002. (Ken Fielding, distributed under a Creative Commons BY-SA 3.0 Licence)

Left: BAe 146-100 G-JEAU at London Heathrow, operating for Air France. (Konstantin von Wedelstaedt, distributed under a Creative Commons GNU FDL 1.2 Licence)

Below: BAe 146-200 G-JEAR operated for Air France from February 1998 to January 2003. (Ken Fielding, distributed under a Creative Commons BY-SA 3.0 Licence)

BAe 146-300 G-JEBA at Paris CDG Airport in August 2001. (Aero Icarus, distributed under a Creative Commons BY-SA 2.0 Licence)

BAe 146-100 G-JEAT at Faro, Portugal, painted in the initial Flybe livery. (Pedro Aragao, distributed under a Creative Commons BY-SA 3.0 Licence)

BAe 146-200 G-JEAJ taxiing out for departure at Manchester Airport. This aircraft left the Flybe fleet in March 2007. (Ken Fielding, distributed under a Creative Commons BY-SA 3.0 Licence)

BAe 146-300 G-JEBB was operated by Jersey European, British European and Flybe for Air France until April 2005. It is shown at Geneva in February 2007 after reverting back to sole use by Flybe. (Aero Icarus, distributed under a Creative Commons BY-SA 2.0 Licence)

Left: BAe 146-300 G-JEBG painted in a special aircraft livery promoting an online gambling site as part of a two-year sponsorship deal from June 2006. (Rob Hodgkins, distributed under a Creative Commons CC BY-SA 2.0 Licence)

Below: British European was to be the launch customer for the new BAe Systems Avro RJX100 airliner. The Avro RJX85 development aircraft G-ORJX was given British European labels to promote the launch customer. (Derek Ferguson)

BAe Systems Avro RJX100 G-6-391, the first and only production RJX100 aircraft, which was due to be delivered to British European in April 2002. (Derek Ferguson)

Right: Bombardier (de Havilland) Dash 8-Q201 G-JEDZ at Aberdeen Airport in July 2001. (Gary Watt, distributed under a Creative Commons GNU FDL 1.2 Licence)

Below: Bombardier (de Havilland) Dash 8-Q311 G-JEDF at Bournemouth. (Les Rickman, distributed under a Creative Commons GNU FDL 1.2 Licence)

Bombardier (de Havilland) Dash 8-Q402 G-JEDJ in British European livery, shortly before the airline was renamed Flybe. This aircraft remained with Flybe until August 2012. (Ken Fielding, distributed under a Creative Commons BY-SA 3.0 Licence)

Left: Bombardier (de Havilland) Dash 8-Q402 G-JECN joined the Flybe fleet in April 2006 and remained with the airline until it went into administration in 2020. (Nigel Richardson)

Below: Bombardier (de Havilland) Dash 8-Q402 G-ECOG departing from Manchester Airport. (Nigel Richardson)

Chapter 4

Expanding the Network

On 5 March 2007, Flybe finally completed the acquisition of British Airways (BA) Connect, a buy-out that was initially announced in November 2006. BA Connect was a regional airline subsidiary of British Airways. It was originally purchased in 1993, becoming BA CitiExpress in 2002, before being renamed BA Connect in 2006. Despite the rebranding and a move to a more 'no-frills approach', the airline lost £27 million in 2004/05 and a further £20 million in 2005/06. Following the takeover, Flybe effectively became the largest regional airline in Europe, doubling its fleet through the acquisition of 39 BA Connect aircraft (28 Embraer ERJ145s, 7 Bombardier Dash 8-Q300s, 4 BAe 146s) and increasing its turnover to £600 million. Flybe's network increased to 152 routes in May 2007, boosting its presence at Birmingham and Manchester airports. British Airways retained BA Connect's operations from London City Airport, operated by the new BA CityFlyer, and received a 15 percent stake in Flybe (through the International Airlines Group (IAG)) in return for £96 million of financial protection for Flybe. This was to cover any cost inefficiencies from operating BA Connect's Embraer ERJ145 aircraft until they could be replaced and any losses resulting from a drop in the future value of these aircraft. The remainder of Flybe's ownership was divided between Rosedale Aviation (69 percent) and Flybe staff (16 percent). Ironically, a number of the inherited aircraft were soon put up for sale by Flybe, after which an order for another 15 Bombardier Dash 8-Q400 aircraft in May 2007, indicated the growing confidence in Flybe's future prospects and its focus on developing a fleet of new and fuel-efficient aircraft.

In July 2007, Flybe launched a new frequent flyer reward scheme called 'Rewards4All', which replaced its previous 'Passport to Freedom' scheme. The new scheme was entirely web based, unlike the previous paper-based scheme, with passengers earning one point for a single journey, two points for a return flight in economy, and double the points in economy plus. The points could be redeemed for flight bookings (for example,16 points for one UK return economy flight or 24 points for a European economy flight) or access to Flybe's executive airport lounges.

An innovative stance taken by Flybe in 2007 was the introduction of an Ecolabel (Environmental Impact Label) rating for each of its aircraft types, similar to that used for electrical items. The rating demonstrated the airline's responsibility to minimise the impact its aircraft had on the environment through noise and gaseous emissions. The Ecolabel provided customers and the general public with information on the noise rating, fuel consumption and emissions (carbon dioxide and nitrogen oxides) for the normal take-off and landing cycle of a flight, and for the total duration of the flight based on distance. The Ecolabels were available to customers on the Flybe website, on the side of aircraft and included with information in the seat pocket. The initiative was praised by the House of Commons Treasury Select Committee, which urged other airlines to follow Flybe's lead. In addition, Flybe painted Dash 8-Q400 G-JEDP in a special green colour scheme to promote its claim to be an environmentally responsible airline.

In January 2008, Flybe announced that Loganair was to be a franchise partner, with Flybe taking over the 'Highlands and Islands' franchise once Loganair's previous arrangement with British Airways had expired. Loganair was founded in 1962. With headquarters in Glasgow, it was serving the Scottish Highlands and Islands, as well as flying routes to Northern Ireland and Dublin. The former British Airways franchise had been in place since 1994, with approximately half a million passengers carried

annually on 26 routes from 16 airports. The new franchise agreement began on 26 October 2008 when Loganair began to operate Saab 340 aircraft in full Flybe livery on more than 50 scheduled routes both within and from Scotland under the Flybe brand, with the potential to carry more than 2.5 million passengers. Under the terms of the agreement, Flybe was not allowed to operate any air services on routes operated by Loganair. A code share agreement with Brussels Airlines also began in November 2008 on routes from Brussels to Birmingham, Bristol and Newcastle, in addition to the arrangements already in place with British Airways and Air France.

As for most of the other major airlines, the financial year 2008/09 was particularly challenging for Flybe. Pre-tax profits dropped from £30.4 million in 2007/08 to £0.1 million, despite an increase in the number of passengers from 7 million to 7.3 million. Losses were largely attributed to a 36 percent increase in fuel costs in the first half of the year (following a doubling of the price of crude oil) and the economic recession (resulting from the global banking crisis), which began to impact the wider business sector in October 2008 with business travel almost being non-existent by January 2009. As a counter-measure, and in negotiation with Bombardier, Flybe restricted its planned fleet growth for

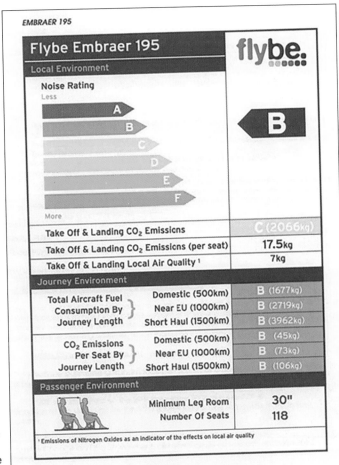

EMBRAER 195

Flybe Embraer 195

flybe.

Local Environment

Noise Rating

Less

A
B
C
D
E
F

More

B

Take Off & Landing CO₂ Emissions		C (2066kg)
Take Off & Landing CO₂ Emissions (per seat)		17.5kg
Take Off & Landing Local Air Quality ¹		7kg

Journey Environment

Total Aircraft Fuel Consumption By Journey Length	Domestic (500km)	B (1677kg)
	Near EU (1000km)	B (2719kg)
	Short Haul (1500km)	B (3962kg)
CO₂ Emissions Per Seat By Journey Length	Domestic (500km)	B (45kg)
	Near EU (1000km)	B (73kg)
	Short Haul (1500km)	B (106kg)

Passenger Environment

	Minimum Leg Room	30"
	Number Of Seats	118

¹ Emissions of Nitrogen Oxides as an indicator of the effects on local air quality

Right: An Ecolabel (Environmental Impact Label) for the Embraer E195. The labels for each aircraft type appeared on the Flybe website, on the side of each aircraft to the left of the forward door, and in the information within the seat pocket. (Flybe)

Below: Bombardier (de Havilland) Dash 8-Q402 G-JEDP, painted in a green livery to publicise Flybe's claim to be the most environmentally neutral operator. (Bjorn Strey, distributed under a Creative Commons CC BY-SA 2.0 Licence)

2009/10 from nine to three Dash 8-Q400 aircraft and reduced its winter 2009 flying programme. A further significant step involved a deal with Olympic Air for that company to take the three new Dash 8-Q400 aircraft due for delivery in 2009, and to purchase two used Dash 8-Q400 aircraft and wet-lease four others (including aircraft, crew and maintenance staff) for one year only from August 2009 to September 2010. In addition, the 39 BA Connect aircraft were to be disposed. These actions prevented any significant staff losses and resulted in a £5.7 million profit by the end of the 2009/10 financial year. The eruption of the Eyjafjallajökull volcano in Iceland which began on 14 April 2010 had a significant impact on Flybe's operations during April and May 2010, and led to a substantial number of flights being cancelled; it ultimately contributed to £11.6 million of lost profit in the 2010/11 financial year.

Flybe's aircraft fleet, in March 2010, consisted of 54 Dash 8-Q400s and 14 Embraer E195s, of which 58 aircraft were on a lease arrangement and only ten actually owned by Flybe. In July 2010, Flybe announced the purchase of 35 Embraer E175 regional jets, which were to be delivered between November 2011 and 2016, with options for a further 65 aircraft. The 88-seat E175 had similar running costs per flight to the slightly smaller (78-seat) Dash 8-Q400 that it was to replace, resulting in a lower cost per seat. The newer aircraft were expected to improve the overall customer experience.

Left: Saab 340B G-LGNB in full Flybe livery and operated by Loganair as part of the franchise agreement between the two airlines. (Ardfern, distributed under a Creative Commons CC BY-SA 3.0 Licence)

Below: Saab 340B G-LGNA at Sumburgh, Shetland in March 2014, operated by Loganair on behalf of Flybe. (Ronnie Robertson, distributed under a Creative Commons CC BY-SA 2.0 Licence)

Above: The Dornier 328-110 was also operated by Loganair for Flybe through the franchise partnership. G-BWWT is shown at Manchester in July 2012. (Nigel Richardson)

Right: Dornier 328-110 G-BYMK in a special livery (Flybe/Loganair) to promote the new route between Dundee and London Stansted introduced in 2014. (Aero Pixels, England, distributed under a Creative Commons CC BY 2.0 Licence)

Towards the end of 2010, Flybe had a network of 215 routes across 73 UK and European airports and comprised a modern fleet of 68 aircraft, with annual passenger numbers of approximately 7.2 million. Flybe was one of only a few European airlines to report profits since the global financial crisis. As a result, the majority shareholder, Rosedale Aviation Holdings, considered it appropriate for Flybe to maximise its growth potential through a flotation on the London Stock Exchange, looking to raise approximately £60 million through new shares. Trading in shares on the Stock Exchange began on the 10 December 2010, with an offer of 20.3 million new shares (28 percent stake in the company) at a price of 295p, valuing the airline at £215 million. A full public release of the remainder of the shares – 'the Global Offer' – took place on the 15 December. Flybe ended its first full week as a listed business with its shares up by 7.5 percent to 317p and went on to raise £66 million for the company. At least 50 percent of the net proceeds from the sale of shares was to be used as capital for funding the aircraft fleet-expansion programme, with the other 50 percent for pursuing additional growth opportunities, such as the expansion of code-share agreements and potential strategic franchise agreements with other European airlines.

During August 2011, Flybe was restructured into three operating divisions: Flybe UK, Flybe Europe and Flybe Aviation Support. The objective was to provide a clearer focus and drive for future business growth and development. The Flybe UK division comprised the UK-domestic and UK-Europe airline businesses; the focus of the Flybe Europe division was airline operations within Europe; and the Flybe Aviation Support division included Flybe's Maintenance, Repair and Overhaul business and the Training Academy. The £24 million Training Academy, based in Exeter, opened in 2011 with financial support from the Learning and Skills Council (£4.3 million) and the UK South West Regional Development Agency (£2.8 million). It featured a flight simulator complex with up to four simulators, cabin crew emergency training facilities, 26 classrooms and workshop facilities. It provided training for both Flybe's workforce and employees of other airlines and organisations, offering courses for aircrew, cabin crew, ground-based, customer-focus personnel and engineers.

Flybe's continued expansion into Europe occurred in 2011, when Finnish Commuter Airlines ('FinnComm') was acquired by Flybe Nordic, a joint venture between Flybe and Finnair. Flybe had a 60 percent share in the partnership, which created the opportunity for Flybe to become the leading regional airline in the Nordic and Baltic region. For Finnair, it created a complementary operator in the Nordic region and a valuable feeder airline for its international operations. Flybe Nordic operated through its subsidiary, Flybe Finland. Equipped with 16 aircraft (three ATR 42-500 and 11 ATR 72-500; and two Embraer E170s leased from Finnair), Flybe Finland's new route network began services on the 30 October 2011 and included Tallinn and Tartu in Estonia, Mariehamn and Trondheim, Norway (an ATR 72-500 was added in October 2012 to replace an ATR 42). Growth of the partnership with Finnair increased in October 2012, when Flybe Finland began to operate a further 12 Embraer E190 aircraft, leased from Finnair, under a contract flying arrangement for Finnair. In total, 28 aircraft were now being flown by Flybe Finland, of which 20 were flying under contract for Finnair.

Partnerships with other European airlines were initiated in 2012, including a two-year deal with Brussels Airlines from 25 March 2012, for whom Flybe were to fly two Dash 8-Q400 aircraft under a similar contract flying agreement to that with Finnair. The aircraft were painted in the Brussels Airlines livery but were operated by Flybe air and cabin crew and maintained by Flybe engineers. The contract was extended in June 2012 to include two more Dash 8-Q400 aircraft, the first of which began operating in September 2012 and the other in late October. In May 2012, Flybe set up a code share arrangement with the Air France-KLM Group on flights to Amsterdam Schiphol Airport (KLM's main hub) and, in January 2012, extended its code share agreement with Air France to include new routes from Aberdeen, Bristol and Newcastle to Paris Charles de Gaulle and from Birmingham to Lyon.

ATR 42-500 OH-ATC at Tallinn, Estonia, in March 2014, operating for Flybe Finland, a joint venture between Flybe and Finnair. (Anna Zvereva, distributed under a Creative Commons CC BY-SA 2.0 Licence)

Painted in the Flybe livery is ATR 72-500 OH-ATE at Tallinn, Estonia in April 2014, operating for Flybe Finland. (Anna Zvereva, distributed under a Creative Commons CC BY-SA 2.0 Licence)

Right: Finnair's Embraer E170-100 OH-LEI at Tallinn in October 2013. The aircraft was leased by Flybe Finland and operated by Flybe crew on behalf of Finnair. (Anna Zvereva, distributed under a Creative Commons CC BY-SA 2.0 Licence)

Below: Bombardier (de Havilland) Dash 8-Q402 G-ECOI operated by Flybe for Brussels Airlines through a contract flying agreement. (Nigel Richardson)

The first four Embraer E175s were delivered to Flybe between 2011 and 2012, together with three new Bombardier Dash 8-Q400 aircraft. In order to minimise any potential financial risk to the business, Flybe took the decision not to increase the size of the aircraft fleet; consequently seven Dash 8-Q400 aircraft were sold to compensate for the new acquisitions and three more were returned to the lessor during 2012.

In April 2012, Manchester Airport became a regional network hub for Flybe. This development increased the choice of domestic flights from the airport, with an affordable choice of multiple day returns throughout the UK. Flybe worked closely with the airport to streamline connectivity, aiming to reduce minimum connecting times to 35 minutes. The hub also provided an alternative to Heathrow for long-haul travel to various destinations. The creation of additional regional connections through Manchester opened up more flights to many parts of the world and the success of the hub was evident in passenger numbers: 9,200 passengers per month were boarding a connecting flight through the airport with Flybe by March 2013, compared to only 2,800 passengers in February 2012 prior to the introduction of the hub.

Despite the positive developments and progress made during 2011 and 2012, these two years were the most challenging financially since Flybe's relaunch and rebranding in 2002. A pre-tax loss of £6.2 million in 2011/12 was succeeded by an almost seven-fold increase to £41.1 million in 2012/13. The main reasons were considered to be fourfold: the state of the UK economy where austerity was impacting on domestic air travel, the impact of increasing Air Passenger Duty on UK domestic passengers, the high cost of aviation fuel, and the depreciation of sterling against the US dollar over a five-year period. In response, Flybe removed 12 loss-making flights from its portfolio and reduced the frequency of flights on some routes. More significantly, in January 2013, the airline announced phase 1 of a turnaround plan, which was expanded in May 2013 with the second phase called 'Making Flybe Fit to Compete', which aimed to return Flybe to profitability and ensure the survival of the business.

Phase 1 included further restructuring of the company into two operating divisions: Flybe UK and Flybe Outsourcing Solutions. Flybe UK continued to focus on UK domestic and UK to Europe operations, while any contract flying activity was now part of the remit of the new Flybe Outsourcing Solutions Division, along with European operations and the activities of the former Aviation Support Division. The success of the partnerships with Finnair and Brussels Airlines had demonstrated the need for effective co-ordination of the outsourcing elements of the former Flybe Europe and Flybe Aviation Support Divisions to third-party customers. Therefore, it seemed logical to integrate both into one division. This ensured that Flybe was well prepared to respond to an anticipated increase in European scheduled contract flying over the next few years. Other significant actions within the first phase of the plan included making cost savings by outsourcing the call centre, on-board catering, line maintenance and ground handling of aircraft. Together with the restructuring, these changes led to the departure of an initial 490 staff, including a 20 percent reduction in the number of management positions.

Phase 2 of the plan involved deferring the delivery of 14 new E175 aircraft from Embraer by three years to 2017–19, which would save £20 million in 2013/14, and, reluctantly, Flybe's 25 arrival/departure paired slots at London Gatwick Airport were sold to easyJet for £20 million.

The Chairman and CEO of Flybe for the previous 20 years, Jim French, stood down from the board in November 2013. Saad Hammad, formerly of easyJet, took over as CEO in August 2013 and Simon Laffin was appointed Chairman in November 2013. At this stage, Hammad implemented a number of immediate actions to accelerate the two phases of the turnaround plan and improve financial performance.

The turnaround plan proved to be successful in returning the business to profitability during 2013/14; a pre-tax profit of £8.1 million and cost savings of £47 million were reported in March 2014.

However, the cost reduction programme led to a number of significant changes to the structure and operation of Flybe. The new, streamlined senior management team removed the company's divisional structure and moved to an integrated organisational structure called One Flybe. More than 1,100 people departed from the company through resignations, transfers to other organisations and a small number of redundancies. The number of UK aircraft bases was reduced from 13 to seven in order to reduce costs; only the larger bases at Belfast, Birmingham, Edinburgh, Exeter, Glasgow, Manchester and Southampton were retained. Despite closure of the smaller bases at Newcastle, Aberdeen, Inverness, Jersey, Guernsey and on the Isle of Man, Flybe continued to operate services from these airports. The rationalisation of Flybe's route network continued into the summer 2014 and included the discontinuation of 30 unprofitable routes and reduced flight frequency on at least 25 other routes. With these measures in place, passenger numbers actually increased slightly to 7.7 million during 2013/14.

By 2014, Flybe had 70 aircraft in its fleet following the delivery of seven E175s since 2012. The 14 E195 aircraft were now considered to be too expensive to operate and surplus to Flybe UK's current route network requirements, hence ten of the aircraft were placed in storage from the end of March 2014. Four aircraft continued to be deployed, although the airline planned to return five to lessors during 2014/15, and was exploring sub-leasing opportunities with a number of airlines for at least six of the remaining aircraft. The options for a further 65 Embraer E175 aircraft, part of the original order announced in

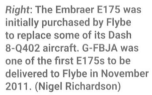

Right: The Embraer E175 was initially purchased by Flybe to replace some of its Dash 8-Q402 aircraft. G-FBJA was one of the first E175s to be delivered to Flybe in November 2011. (Nigel Richardson)

Below: Embraer E175 G-FBJB at Manchester in September 2014. (Nigel Richardson)

July 2010, were cancelled in November 2013. Two of the four Dash 8-Q400s, which had been operating for Brussels Airlines since 2012, returned to Flybe in March 2014 and the remaining two were due to complete their flying contracts by the end of October 2014, although this was extended by one year.

April 2014 saw a full relaunch of the Flybe brand, including the marketing tagline 'The fastest way from A to Flybe' and the slogan 'Faster than road or rail' on the side of the aircraft engines in order to target rail and road users and highlight the speed with which the airline was able to get them to a destination as a key part of its marketing strategy. The relaunch featured purple as the new brand colour, with a redesigned website and advertising materials. The new aircraft livery featured a predominantly purple fuselage, wings and engines, which was separated from the white vertical stabiliser carrying the Flybe logo by yellow and red stripes. There was also a purple-themed cabin crew uniform. The focus was very much on this being a new era for Flybe, with a renewed commitment to customer service and to delivering an excellent customer experience. In order that everyone involved with the airline was on board with the new brand, all employees and business partners were required to take an induction programme on 'The Purple Way' followed by a 'Flybe Loves Service' training programme. Flybe's strategy now focused on two key business areas for development: first, to continue as a regional branded airline providing scheduled regional connectivity across the UK and services to some European destinations and, second, to build new contract flying partnerships (so-called 'white label' partnerships) and franchise agreements.

In the relaunch of the Flybe brand in April 2014, purple was included as the new brand colour. Bombardier (de Havilland) Dash 8-Q402 G-PRPA displays the new purple aircraft livery. (Nigel Richardson)

Embraer E195 G-FBEJ in a special version of Flybe's purple livery to promote Yorkshire. The special livery, launched in 2016, was developed as part of a partnership between Doncaster Sheffield Airport and Welcome to Yorkshire. (Rob Hodgkins, distributed under a Creative Commons CC BY-SA 2.0 Licence)

A consideration of the network showed that many routes involved short flights from regional airports on which there were too few passengers to operate a standard jet profitably, such as an Airbus A320 or Boeing 737. At some airports, the runways were also too short for the effective operation of these aircraft. These routes were less attractive to established airlines and low-cost carriers but well suited to Flybe's smaller Dash 8-Q400 aircraft. Also, by extending its range of code share partnerships, Flybe was able to provide trouble-free transfers onto long-haul, international routes from regional airports. Nine new routes were launched in 2014, including seven from Birmingham to Alicante, Bordeaux, Cologne, Florence, Palma, Porto and Toulouse, and two from Newquay to Birmingham and London Southend. A five-year deal was signed with London City Airport for Flybe to begin operating services from there again. The services began in October 2014, operating Dash 8-Q400 aircraft to and from Edinburgh, Belfast, Dublin, Inverness and Exeter, with plans for future services to European ski resorts and destinations in France and northern Spain.

A franchise agreement with Stobart Air (the new name for the Irish regional airline, Aer Arann), was announced in March 2014, which included seven routes from London Southend to Antwerp, Rennes, Caen, Munster Osnabruck, Cologne, Bonn and Groningen, with the potential to accommodate additional routes, if required. Stobart Air initially operated two ATR 72-500 aircraft on behalf of Flybe from June 2014, painted in Flybe's new purple livery. Stobart Air also operated services on behalf of Aer Lingus as part of another franchising agreement.

In October 2014, Flybe became part of the Avios Travel Rewards Programme, bringing to an end its 'Rewards4All' frequent flyer scheme. The new partnership with Avios was considered to be a significant service enhancement for Flybe customers, offering a wider range of reward opportunities.

Despite showing some recovery in 2014, Flybe's end-of-year financial results announced in March 2015, showed a further slump to a pre-tax loss of £35.6 million. The Turnaround and Transformation Plan had been in place for 18 months and despite the overall losses, there had been significant progress in reducing costs, which had continued during 2014/15. The Flybe Finland partnership was not meeting Flybe's expectation of profit-generation, with much of the poor performance due to scheduled flying operations rather than contract flying for Finnair. In March 2015, Flybe sold its share in Flybe Finland to Finnair for a mere one euro to avoid further substantial losses. The problematic legacy of the costly Embraer E195 jets still remained. Four aircraft were returned to the lessor in early 2015 and a further one in July 2015. Two aircraft continued to operate for Flybe on high-demand routes from Birmingham and Manchester but seven aircraft remained temporarily grounded, contributing significantly to the loss burden due to lease payments.

More positive developments during 2014/15 included the signing of a deal with Bombardier to upgrade the airline's 48 Dash 8-Q400 aircraft in order to improve technical reliability. Flybe also successfully resolved the contractual agreement with Embraer, without penalties, with regard to the outstanding 24 E175 aircraft out of the original order of 35. As part of the resolution, Flybe agreed to receive four of the 24 E175s in 2018, with the remaining 20 going to Republic Holdings. In a reciprocal arrangement, Flybe agreed to sub-lease 24 used Dash 8-Q400s from Republic Airways for delivery between 2015 and 2019, and with considerably lower leasing rates than Flybe was currently paying for its existing Dash 8 aircraft. Flybe also purchased five of its current Dash 8-Q400s, which were due for return to the lessor, to provide capacity for the expansion of operations from London City Airport.

During 2014/15, Flybe applied its route assessment model to 362 routes, which led to the closure of 24 loss-making regional routes but the opening of 26 new routes. Flybe re-opened its base at Aberdeen in late 2014, basing four Dash 8-Q400 aircraft at the airport to operate seven routes, including those to Leeds/Bradford, Southampton, London City and Jersey. Bournemouth was opened as a new base in March 2015, where Flybe based two Dash 8-Q400s to fly ten new routes, including those to Glasgow,

Dublin, Jersey, Manchester, Amsterdam, Paris and several other locations in northern France. Cardiff Airport also opened as a new Flybe base in the summer of 2015 where two Embraer E195s were based, with new routes added to the existing network including Cardiff to Cork, Dublin, Edinburgh, Glasgow, Munich, Milan and Paris.

In June 2015, Emirates announced a new code-share agreement with Flybe which augmented 25 Flybe routes across the UK and provided Flybe customers with connectivity onto Emirates flights to Dubai from Manchester, Glasgow and Birmingham.

A six-year agreement with Scandinavian airline SAS for a new regional 'white label' (contract-flying) programme at Stockholm was signed in early 2015. Initially Flybe leased four ATR 72-600 aircraft to operate short-haul services in Europe on behalf of SAS from October 2015, with the lease of another ATR 72 in April 2016. In addition, the contract flying for Brussels Airlines involving the use of two Dash 8-Q400 aircraft was extended for another two years from October 2015.

Left: A franchise agreement between Flybe and Stobart Air began in June 2014. One of the first aircraft operated by Stobart Air for Flybe was ATR 72-500 EI-REM. (Nigel Richardson)

Below: ATR 72-500 EI-REL at Manchester in August 2016, operated by Stobart Air for Flybe. (Nigel Richardson)

Above: Flybe leased five ATR 72-600s from 2015–2016 to operate flights on behalf of SAS. One of those aircraft was G-FBXC. (Bene Riobo, distributed under a Creative Commons CC BY-SA 4.0 Licence)

Right: ATR 72-600 G-FBXE operated by Flybe for SAS between April 2016 and February 2019. (Bene Riobo, distributed under a Creative Commons CC BY-SA 4.0 Licence)

Back in November 2014, Flybe Aviation Services (FAS) was created as a stand-alone entity encompassing the maintenance, repair and overhaul business. FAS was successful in gaining an eight-and-a-half year contract with Airbus for airframe-related maintenance, repair and overhaul of the RAF's new fleet of Airbus A400M Atlas aircraft, which commenced delivery in November 2014. This required FAS to set up a dedicated facility at RAF Brize Norton, the base of the A400M aircraft.

Towards the end of 2015, Flybe announced that it had completed 'Project Blackbird', an internal network study looking at options to deploy the nine Embraer E195 aircraft, which were surplus to requirements. During 2016, two of these aircraft were to be based at Cardiff, one at Exeter and two at Doncaster Sheffield as part of a long-term agreement with these airports, flying to a mix of destinations across the UK, and to cities and regional centres in mainland Europe. One aircraft became based at Newquay, replacing a Bombardier Dash 8-Q400, as part of a public service obligation with Cornwall Council to satisfy the increased demand on the Newquay to London Gatwick route. Of the remaining three aircraft, one was redeployed to Birmingham and one to Manchester, operating high-load factor routes as they had done during 2015; one aircraft remained on standby. It was predicted that these arrangements would provide Flybe with a £40 million saving, equal to half of the cost obligation over the remaining term of the aircraft leases. Further cost savings were achieved in February 2016 through the outright purchase of three Dash 8-Q400 aircraft from the operating lease, in line with a strategy to rebalance the aircraft fleet away from lease arrangements in order to achieve ownership of at least 50 percent of the fleet.

On the same day that Flybe confirmed it had resolved the Embraer E195 issue, the announcement was made to withdraw from Bournemouth Airport, just eight months after opening a base there. Flybe's south coast operation was eventually consolidated at Southampton Airport, although the jet aircraft based there were withdrawn.

Further network development took place during 2015/16 when 52 new routes were launched, of which only 14 percent had a competitive airline. The new routes focused on connecting more regional bases in the UK to cities in Europe, including Rotterdam, Dusseldorf, Amsterdam, Paris and Milan, as well as some additional domestic routes including Edinburgh–Liverpool and Exeter–Glasgow. A code share agreement with Virgin Atlantic, launched in April 2016, allowed passengers from 12 of Flybe's domestic routes and seven of its UK–Europe routes to connect onto 15 Virgin Atlantic routes to the US and the Caribbean from Manchester, Glasgow and Gatwick airports. With the addition of Virgin Atlantic, Flybe now had nine code share partnerships, including Cathay Pacific, Emirates, Aer Lingus and Air France. Flybe's first intra-European flights were launched on 1 August 2016 from Hanover to Milan and Lyon using Dash 8-Q400 aircraft. Unfortunately, the Lyon route proved unsuccessful and was axed in January 2017.

Additional network developments through a new franchise agreement with Blue Islands operated flights initially linking Jersey and Southampton on behalf of Flybe from June 2016, and later included Jersey to London City and Guernsey to Southampton. Blue Islands painted an ATR 42-500 and three ATR 72-500 aircraft in the Flybe livery and, as with Flybe's other franchise agreements, employed all of its own crew, maintained its own aircraft and controlled its own handling arrangements.

During 2015/2016, Flybe achieved profitability once more, reporting a pre-tax profit of £2.7 million. After almost three years of the transformation plan, Flybe considered the business to be much more financially resilient and was anticipating a period of moderately profitable growth going forward, through a controlled expansion into Europe, with the ultimate aim of once again becoming Europe's leading regional airline. Much of the recovery had been led by the CEO, Saad Hammad, so it was particularly unexpected when he stood down from the role with immediate effect at the end of October 2016. The news led to a 15 percent drop in the price of the company's shares, down to 37p, although the share price had been progressively declining from 90p at the end of 2015.

A franchise agreement between Flybe and Blue Islands commenced in June 2016. Painted in Flybe's purple livery is Blue islands' ATR 42-500 G-ISLF. (flybyeigenjeer, distributed under a Creative Commons CC BY-SA 2.0 Licence)

Above: ATR 72-500 G-ISLL of Blue Islands, operating on behalf of Flybe, landing at Bristol in September 2017. (Kev Slade)

Right: Embraer ERJ145 G-ERJC at Manchester Airport in August 2007. (MilborneOne, distributed under a Creative Commons GNU FDL 1.2 Licence)

Below: Saab 340B G-LGNF turning onto final approach to Sumburgh Airport, Shetland. (Ronnie Robertson, distributed under a Creative Commons CC BY-SA 2.0 Licence)

Loganair's Saab 2000 G-LGNR at Manchester in May 2017, operating for Flybe. (Nigel Richardson)

Saab 2000 G-LGNO in the original Flybe colour scheme, operated by Loganair on behalf of Flybe. (James, distributed under a Creative Commons CC BY-SA 2.0 Licence)

Bombardier (de Havilland) Dash 8-Q402 G-ECOK was operated by Flybe for Brussels Airlines between October 2012 and October 2017. (Nigel Richardson)

Embraer E195 G-FBEC at Faro in June 2008. (Pedro Aragao, distributed under a Creative Commons CC BY-SA 3.0 Licence)

Above: The final Embraer E195 to be delivered to Flybe was G-FBEN, pictured at Manchester in September 2016. (Nigel Richardson)

Below left: The cockpit of Embraer E195 G-F-BEM. (Fergus Bell)

Below right: The seating configuration in the cabin of Embraer E195 G-F-BEM. (Fergus Bell)

Left: Passenger seating on board Embraer E195 G-FBEK. (Neil McDonald)

Below: Embraer E175 G-FBJE departs from Manchester in June 2015. (Nigel Richardson)

Bottom: Embraer E175 G-FBJI taxies in at Manchester in 2014. The Embraer E175 can accommodate 76 passengers in a two-class seating configuration. (Nigel Richardson)

Dornier 328-110 G-CCGS of Loganair, operating on behalf of Flybe, at Manchester in September 2016. (Nigel Richardson)

ATR 72-500 EI-REL at Manchester in August 2015. (Nigel Richardson)

ATR 72-500 OH-ATI operating for Flybe Finland in April 2014. (Anna Zvereva, distributed under a Creative Commons CC BY-SA 2.0 Licence)

De Havilland DHC-6-310 Twin Otter G-BVVK of Loganair, operating for Flybe in May 2017. (Ronnie Macdonald, distributed under a Creative Commons CC BY 2.0 Licence)

Loganair's de Havilland DHC-6-310 Twin Otter G-BZFP on Barra Beach, Outer Hebrides, Scotland in 2010, operating for Flybe. (calflier001, distributed under a Creative Commons CC BY-SA 2.0 Licence)

Chapter 5
Takeover Then Demise

At the beginning of 2017, former CityJet Chief Executive, Christine Ourmières-Widener, was appointed CEO of Flybe. One of the first major issues she had to deal with was a pre-tax loss of £48.5 million in the financial year to the end of March 2017, despite revenue rising by 13.4 percent to £707.4 million. Flybe's fleet had grown significantly since March 2015, reaching a peak of 85 aircraft in May 2017 (including five ATR 72s operated on behalf of SAS). The fleet growth was partly inadvertent as a result of the company's inability to dispose of any of the nine surplus Embraer E195 aircraft. The rest was due to the delivery of eight Bombardier Dash 8-Q400 aircraft from Republic Airways as part of the deal with Embraer to cancel part of the Embraer E175 order, which resulted in a growth in seat capacity. However, increases in passenger numbers in both 2015/16 (6.4 percent) and 2016/17 (7.6 percent) were insufficient to compensate for the increased capacity. Flybe's load factor (the percentage of available seating filled with passengers) declined from 75.2 percent in 2015 to 69.6 percent in 2017. Although the amount of revenue per passenger remained relatively steady, the decline in the load factor caused the amount of passenger revenue per seat to fall by 1.4 percent in the financial year 2016 and by 3.6 percent in the financial year 2017.

In addition to the over-capacity problems, a major upgrade to Flybe's IT systems, costing almost £5 million, contributed to the financial loss in 2017, with further expenditure of £6–10 million anticipated in 2017/18 for IT systems development work.

In response to the company's financial problems, the new CEO developed a sustainable business improvement plan, embedding a clear strategy about returning to the core business of the airline, which had been successful in the past. The plan focused on six key areas:

1. Sales and marketing, to drive sustainable revenue growth and maximise profitability. An enhanced digital e-commerce platform was part of this focus area.
2. Network and fleet optimisation, leading to a tighter and profitable flight network and a long-term fleet configuration to meet the requirements of the airline.
3. Operational excellence/performance, including improvements in reliability and on-time performance to meet customer expectations, especially in a demand-driven network.
4. Organisational excellence, including the design and implementation of a cost-effective organisation structure with clear performance indicators embedded within the job roles of all employees.
5. Technology, with investment in core operational IT platforms to improve the digital online experience for passengers and the support systems for Flybe's operations and engineering teams.
6. Cost-improvement programme, to identify where costs could be reduced at all levels in the business without impacting on performance and the quality of services to customers.

A significant amount of improvement was achieved during 2017/18: the number of passengers using Flybe increased by 7.7 percent to 9.5 million and the load factor improved from 69.6 percent in 2016/17 to 75.6 percent in 2017/18. Nine new routes were offered and 14 routes were cut in response to a clear focus on profitable flying. Flybe's new routes included flights from London Heathrow to Aberdeen and Edinburgh from March 2017, taking over valuable 'remedy' slots previously used by

Virgin Atlantic Little Red, and flights from Cardiff to Rome, and Aberdeen to Southampton as part of the winter schedule. The franchise agreement with Loganair ended on 31 August 2017; Flybe stated the reasons as a failure to agree on future operational standards and commercial arrangements.

Flybe opened its first European crew base at Dusseldorf Airport on 1 February 2017. The airline already served Dusseldorf with flights from Birmingham, Cardiff, Doncaster Sheffield, Manchester and Southampton. In preparation for the opening, Flybe recruited new pilots and cabin crew, together with engineering support for the two Dash 8-Q400 aircraft that were to be based at Dusseldorf. The existing code share agreement between Flybe and Air Berlin provided opportunities for customers on Flybe's Dusseldorf routes to feed onto Air Berlin flights from its Dusseldorf hub to Scandinavia, Poland, Italy, France, Austria and Switzerland, as well as other cities within Germany.

Further network optimisation was achieved through a new five-year franchise agreement and joint venture alliance with Eastern Airways to operate flights in Scotland under the Flybe brand in direct competition with Loganair. The Flybe/Eastern joint alliance started on 1 September 2017, with Eastern

Left: Flybe returns to Heathrow in March 2017 with daily flights to Edinburgh and Aberdeen. (Flybe)

Below: Bombardier (de Havilland) Dash 8-Q402 G-PRPL at London Heathrow. G-PRPL provided Flybe's inaugural flight between London Heathrow and Aberdeen on 26 March 2017. (John Taggart, distributed under a Creative Commons CC BY-SA 2.0 Licence)

Airways operating four aircraft on six of Flybe's existing Scottish routes from Aberdeen, Glasgow and Edinburgh on the mainland to Stornoway, Kirkwall and Sumburgh. The franchise flight network, which began on 28 October 2017, was more wide-ranging and included flights between Aberdeen, Glasgow, Newcastle, Stornoway, Durham Tees Valley, Leeds/Bradford, Humberside, Belfast City, the Isle of Man, Anglesey, Cardiff, Norwich, Southampton, Paris Orly and Rodez. In addition, the franchise agreement with Stobart was extended from May 2017, with flights to 12 destinations from London Southend Airport, including Budapest, Milan and Venice. Meanwhile, the contract flying arrangement with Brussels Airlines ended in October 2017.

Bombardier (de Havilland) Dash 8-Q402 G-PRPI was delivered to Flybe in September 2016. This Dash 8-Q402 aircraft was sub-leased from Republic Airlines by Flybe as part of a deal with Embraer to cancel some of its Embraer E175 order. (Nigel Richardson)

Bombardier (de Havilland) Dash 8-Q402 G-PRPJ at Manchester in April 2017, another sub-leased aircraft from Republic Airlines. (Nigel Richardson)

Eastern Airways operated BAe Jetstream 41 G-MAJK as part of the joint alliance/franchise with Flybe, which started in September 2017. (Ronnie Robertson, distributed under a Creative Commons CC BY-SA 2.0 Licence)

Embraer E170-100 G-CIXV operating a Flybe-Eastern Airways joint alliance flight to Sumburgh, Shetland in September 2017. (Ronnie Robertson, distributed under a Creative Commons CC BY-SA 2.0 Licence)

A comprehensive review of the aircraft fleet during 2017 indicated that the Bombardier Dash 8-Q400 was the most suitable aircraft for Flybe's current and future needs, together with a small number of Embraer E175s for the longer and busier routes. There was some progress in reducing the overall fleet size, with the return of five Dash 8-Q400s at the end of their lease and two Embraer E195s (G-FBEF and G-FBEH) being leased to Stobart Air from November 2017 until late 2018. Delivery of the four outstanding Embraer E175s from the original order was scheduled to begin in 2018 but was delayed until July 2019 at Flybe's request.

At the end of the 2017–18 financial year, Flybe recorded a reduced net loss of £9.4 million (compared to a loss of £48.5 million in 2016/17) and a £52.2 million increase in revenue to £752.6 million, which indicated that the initial stages of the sustainable business improvement plan had delivered a significantly improved commercial performance. The loss was now mainly due to maintenance costs, contract charges associated with the digital platform investment and the weather conditions during February and March 2018, which caused the cancellation of 994 flights.

In February 2018, the Stobart Group, owner of franchise partner Stobart Air, confirmed an interest in a takeover bid of Flybe. A number of potential structures were considered from a non-controlling interest through to the acquisition of 100 percent of Flybe. The announcement by the Stobart Group led to shares in Flybe increasing by 36 percent to 47p. However, Flybe rejected the proposed bid and, after failing to reach any satisfactory agreement, the Stobart Group withdrew its interest in the company in March 2018, which resulted in the share price falling by 25 percent to around 35p.

Flybe unveiled a new, streamlined aircraft livery in September 2018, with a white front section of the fuselage separated from a purple rear fuselage and vertical stabiliser by a broad lilac band to replace the yellow and red stripes associated with the former British European. The new livery reflected the 'Close to You' brand, which was originally introduced in 2017 to highlight the fact that Flybe was closer to its customers than other airlines because of its operating presence at a number of regional airports. The plan was to roll out the new livery across the entire fleet, with priority to be given to aircraft still painted in the old blue and white livery but, in the end, only one Dash 8-Q400 aircraft (G-JECP) was repainted.

Flybe introduced a new purple livery in September 2018, however, only one aircraft, Bombardier (de Havilland) Dash 8-Q402 G-JECP, was repainted to match the brand change. (Markus Eigenheer, distributed under a Creative Commons CC BY-SA 2.0 Licence)

Bombardier (de Havilland) Dash 8-Q402 G-JECP in the new purple livery at London Heathrow in March 2019. (John Taggart, distributed under a Creative Commons CC BY-SA 2.0 Licence)

Further reductions in fleet size occurred during 2018: two E195s were withdrawn from service, one being returned to the lessor, together with a Dash 8-Q400. Nevertheless, Flybe introduced a small number of new routes at the same time, including Belfast City to Doncaster Sheffield and Cardiff to Venice.

A profit warning was issued by Flybe in October 2018 when the group predicted a full-year pre-tax loss of £22 million. This was underpinned by increased fuel costs, a weak pound and a weakened customer demand for travel in the UK and Europe, and mindful of the approaching winter period and its associated diminished demand. Further financial strain on Flybe resulted from the uncertainty caused by Brexit, in particular the unknown impact a no-deal Brexit scenario would have on the aviation industry. Credit card providers were asking for more financial security from Flybe. They began to withhold cash from some advanced ticket sales until after the flight, which meant less cash flow and operating capital for the airline. The six-month interim financial results published in November indicated that revenue was down by 2.4 percent to £419.2 million. The airline was now valued at approximately £25 million, a fraction of the £215 million valuation in 2010 on entry to the Stock Exchange. The share price had fallen by almost 75 percent since September 2018 to 11p.

The worrying half-yearly results prompted Flybe to announce that it was reviewing its strategic options, including the possibility of selling the business. Other options included focusing only on profitable routes; unprofitable routes would be withdrawn and further capacity and cost-saving measures would be implemented to address the challenges facing the airline. On 22 November 2018, it was revealed that Virgin Atlantic had been in discussion with Flybe concerning a possible takeover. Flybe's valuable take-off and landing slots at Heathrow were of particular interest to Virgin Atlantic, as

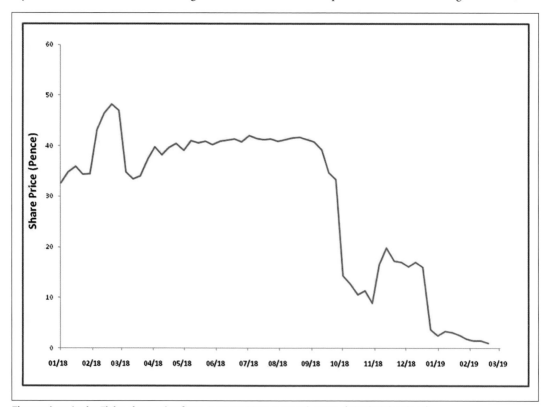

Fluctuations in the Flybe share price from January 2018 to March 2019. (Nigel Richardson)

was the potential of using Flybe's regional network to feed passengers into Virgin Atlantic's long-haul operations at Manchester, London Heathrow and Gatwick Airport. Flybe was already feeding some passengers onto a number of Virgin Atlantic's international flights through a code share agreement between the two carriers. Other airlines that were reported to be interested in purchasing Flybe included the Stobart Group, after its failed attempt earlier in the year, and British Airways, through its owner, the International Airlines Group (IAG). News of a potential takeover led to an almost immediate 50 percent rise in the value of Flybe's shares.

Flybe also received a valuable cash injection of £4.5 million in January 2019 from the sale of a number of take-off and landing slots at Gatwick Airport to IAG for use by Vueling. The slots had been used for the Gatwick-Newquay service, which Flybe moved to London Heathrow from March 2019. Two additional new routes from Heathrow to the Isle of Man and Guernsey were added.

Despite further discussions, it wasn't until 11 January 2019 that a formal takeover bid for Flybe, worth £2.2 million (1p per share), was made by the Connect Airways Consortium. Connect Airways was a joint venture company formed in December 2018 by Virgin Atlantic Ltd, Stobart Aviation (a subsidiary of the Stobart Group) and Cyrus Capital Partners through DLP Holdings. Virgin Atlantic and Stobart Aviation each had a 30 percent share in the consortium, while Cyrus Capital held the remaining 40 percent. The initial bid involved the consortium agreeing to provide Flybe with an advanced bridging loan of £20 million to continue operations. It also included a takeover of Stobart Air, which at the time was in a franchise agreement with Flybe. On completion of the proposed acquisition, Flybe was to receive a further £80 million. Both Flybe and Stobart Air were to retain their Air Operators Certificates but were to operate under the Virgin Atlantic Brand. Subject to shareholder and legal approval, the takeover deal was expected to be completed by the summer of 2019. However, after consideration of the bid, Flybe felt that it would be unable to meet the conditions of the bridging loan. Four days later, Connect returned with an improved and restructured offer of £2.8 million together with improved bridging loan conditions, in which it would acquire Flybe (including Flybe Aviation Services) and the Flybe.com digital company.

Flybe accepted Connect's revised offer to ensure the security of the airline, its employees, partners and shareholders. Flybe was to receive £10 million immediately, with another £10 million available, if required, and a further £100 million on a secured loan basis on completion of the takeover. It was suggested that, without the bridging loan, Flybe was only a few days away from collapse. The decision angered Flybe's shareholders, especially since earlier that year the Flybe board had rejected a takeover approach by the Stobart Group when the airline was valued at approximately 40p per share. Now they were being offered only 1p per share. However, approval of the takeover bid by shareholders was not required because they had previously (December 2019) approved Flybe's decision to transfer shares from a premium to a standard listing on the London Stock Exchange, on the understanding that it would make it easier for the company to dispose of some of its assets, if necessary, to restore cash balances. The offset was that shareholders didn't get a vote on business transactions, such as the takeover deal.

One of the largest shareholders, Hosking Partners, with a 19 percent share holding in Flybe, challenged the proposed takeover deal, suggesting that the £2.8 million offer didn't reflect the true value of the airline. Hoskings alleged that the manner of the proposed sale blocked rival offers of a higher value. An alternative bid, considered by the Flybe board, was received from former Stobart CEO, Andrew Tinkler. The bid, which included capital injection, was rejected on 4 February 2019 on the grounds that it offered insufficient certainty to secure Flybe's future. The American Airlines-backed Mesa Air Group, with support from Hosking Partners and Andrew Tinkler, then submitted a conditional contingency proposal to invest £65 million of new equity into Flybe, equivalent to 4.5p per share, followed by potential asset sales, which would provide up to £120 million of new funding for Flybe. The proposal was rejected by Flybe on the 20 February, as it did not think it could be completed in the timeframe required for the airline to continue trading. The following day, Flybe announced the completion of the sale of Flybe Ltd and Flybe.com to Connect Airways. The sale of the parent company, Flybe Group plc, now an empty company following the sale of its trading entities, was confirmed by its shareholders on 4 March 2019 and removed from the Stock Exchange on 11 March 2019.

Following the takeover, it was expected that Connect Airways' priorities would be to review the number of services operated by Flybe and to ensure that they were aligned to provide improved connectivity with Virgin Atlantic's long-haul operations. This raised questions about the future of Flybe's code share agreements with other airlines, some of which competed with Virgin Atlantic on international routes. Following a review of business performance, Flybe discontinued the use of Embraer E175/E195 aircraft from Doncaster Sheffield, Cardiff, Exeter and Norwich at the end of the summer of 2019. The consequences were the closure of Doncaster Sheffield and Cardiff as Flybe bases and the withdrawal of a significant number of routes from the four airports. Some routes from Manchester and Southampton were also closed.

In October 2019, Flybe began a code share agreement with Loganair, which covered 19 routes flown by Flybe (including Aberdeen, Belfast City, Inverness, Birmingham, Cardiff, Edinburgh, Glasgow, Exeter, Southampton, Jersey, Glasgow and Manchester), thereby extending its UK network. However, the size of the aircraft fleet and problems of over-capacity remained. Four E195s were withdrawn during 2019 leaving only two operational. Two E175s were withdrawn in November 2019 and the five ATR 72-600s previously operated on behalf of SAS were leased to Loganair.

At this stage, it was announced that Flybe was to be rebranded as Virgin Connect as early as the beginning of 2020, with the airline saying goodbye to purple and hello to red. The focus was on Virgin Connect becoming Europe's most favoured and successful regional airline, providing customers with the same high-quality travel experience as other Virgin-related brands.

However, early in January 2020, Flybe was once again in financial difficulties, and faced increasing losses despite the bridging loans from Connect Airways. Flybe had been trying to secure additional funding without success, leading to an accounting firm (Ernst & Young) being put on stand-by to deal with the possibility of Flybe going into administration. The Department for Transport and the Department for Business, Energy and Industrial Strategy, began to explore the possibility of providing or facilitating some emergency financial support for Flybe as part of a rescue deal. The government was concerned about the impact a collapse of Flybe would have on smaller airports and UK regional connectivity, particularly as

A concept image of a Bombardier (de Havilland) Dash 8-Q402 in a Virgin Atlantic livery that may have resulted following rebranding of Flybe as Virgin Connect. (Trent Nickson)

improving regional connectivity was a manifesto commitment as part of the 'levelling up' programme. A deal was finally agreed on 15 January 2020, including a potential loan of up to £100 million and/or a possible short-term deferred payment plan for an outstanding Air Passenger Duty debt from December 2019. The deal also required the Connect Airways shareholders to provide an additional £30 million of funding. In addition, the government agreed to conduct an urgent review of regional transport connectivity, focusing in particular on issues concerning Air Passenger Duty on domestic flights. Flybe had been challenging Air Passenger Duty charges for a number of years as the airline was paying £26 on a return domestic fare while the duty on a European flight from the UK was only £13. The proposed deal, especially the deferral of payment of outstanding Air Passenger Duty, received criticism from the aviation industry, in particular from the CEOs of IAG and Ryanair, the latter threatening legal action. The government was cautious in its approach, consulting with the European Commission amid concerns about the legitimacy of the deal in relation to competition and state-aid rules.

Believing that it had been saved from administration, Flybe began to outline its future plans under the Virgin Connect brand, including a return to London Gatwick of the Public Service Obligation link to Newquay. The released slots at Heathrow from the transfer of the Newquay service were to be used for flights to Dusseldorf. Flybe's planned summer schedule for 2020 included seven new routes: six from Southend to Belfast, Edinburgh, Glasgow, Newcastle, Isle of Man and Jersey, operated by three of Flybe's Dash 8-Q400s and two ATR 72-600s from partner Stobart Air, and one between Manchester and Stuttgart.

The outbreak of the Covid-19 pandemic in late-February 2020 and its impact on the aviation industry and business travel amplified Flybe's ongoing financial problems, with a sudden 30–40 percent downturn in flight bookings. Two of the Connect shareholders, Virgin Atlantic and Stobart Aviation, informed Flybe that they were no longer able to provide further funding as a result of the impact of Covid-19 on its own bookings. Flybe had approximately £5.7 million of available cash, with payments due to creditors of more than £10 million. The company was unable to pay its debts. Following withdrawal of the of the Government's offer of a £100 million loan, a decision partly influenced by concerns around the impact of the coronavirus outbreak, the airline filed for administration on 5 March 2020 and ceased operations with immediate effect. The collapse led to more than 2,000 jobs being lost.

At the time it went into administration, Flybe had 65 aircraft in its fleet: 54 Dash 8-Q400s, nine Embraer E175s and two Embraer E195s. Flybe owned 20 of the Dash 8-Q400s and one E175, the remaining 44 aircraft were on operating leases. Flybe had never taken delivery of the four E175s, which were scheduled for delivery from mid-2019. Only 15 of the 24 Dash 8-Q400s due to be sub-leased from Republic Airlines as part of the E175 deal with Embraer were delivered.

Flybe's website was no longer accessible for bookings on the evening of the 4 March 2020, prior to the company going into administration. (Flybe)

Flybe

Flybe Limited (in Administration) ('the Company' or 'Flybe')
THIS PAGE WILL NOT BE MONITORED

Flybe entered Administration on 5 March 2020 and Alan Hudson, Joanne Robinson, Lucy Winterborne and Simon Edel of EY have been appointed as Joint Administrators.

All flights have been grounded and the UK business has ceased trading with immediate effect.

Customers

If you are due to fly with Flybe, please DO NOT TRAVEL TO THE AIRPORT unless you have arranged an alternative flight with another airline. Please note that Flybe is unfortunately not able to arrange alternative flights for passengers.

If you have a booking sold by another airline that includes travel on a Flybe flight, please contact the relevant airline or travel agent to confirm if there is any impact to your travel plans.

Customers are also advised to monitor the Civil Aviation Authority website for further information www.caa.co.uk/news

If you require any further information or assistance, please contact the Administrators by email at flybeadministration@uk.ey.com.

Employees

In the event that you were an employee of the Company and you require any further information or assistance in relation to the Administration, please contact the Administrators by email at flybeemployees@uk.ey.com.

Creditors and suppliers

In the event that you were a supplier or creditor of the Company and you require further details in relation to the Administration, please direct your enquiries to the Administrators' office by email at flybesuppliers@uk.ey.com.

Media

All media enquiries are directed to contact flybepressenquiries@uk.ey.com.

Notification of Administration on the Company website, 5 March 2020. (Flybe)

The impact of Flybe's collapse on some regional airports was highly significant; at Southampton Airport almost 95 percent of the passengers on scheduled flights used Flybe, and high percentages of flights were operated by Flybe at other airports, including Exeter (78 percent), Belfast City (77 percent), Newquay (65 percent) and 40–50 percent at Cardiff, Jersey, Guernsey, the Isle of Man and Teeside. Flybe's franchise partners continued to operate following the company's demise. Blue Islands maintained the operation of its flights from Jersey and Guernsey to Bristol, Southampton, London City, East Midlands and Newquay, and even increased the frequency of flights on the more popular routes. Similarly, Eastern Airways continued with its operations, adding three new routes between Aberdeen and Birmingham, Southampton and Manchester, and Southampton and Newcastle. Former franchise partner Loganair continued to operate 16 of its Flybe code-share routes and also introduced a number of new routes to cover the shortfall, including those to Belfast City, Manchester, Birmingham, Cardiff, Exeter, Southampton and Jersey from its bases at Aberdeen, Edinburgh, Glasgow, Inverness and Newcastle.

Chapter 6
Flybe Flies Again

Following the collapse of Flybe, the Civil Aviation Authority (CAA) proposed to suspend or revoke Flybe's operating licence, Air Operators Certificate and its related routes licences. However, the administrators believed that the business and at least some of the assets could be sold as a going concern and continued to pursue this recommendation, challenging the decision by the CAA as it would undermine their attempts to sell the company. Although the CAA went ahead and revoked the Operating Licence, it was forced to withdraw its decision following a successful appeal by the Administrators to the Secretary of State for Transport, Grant Shapps.

As well as marketing the business, the Administrators explored the disposal of valuable assets. The aircraft that Flybe had been purchasing via loans from finance companies were reclaimed by the financiers. No substantial offers for the aircraft were received due to the market for buying and selling aircraft being depressed as a result of the impact of Covid-19 on the aviation industry. Ultimately, all leased aircraft were returned to the respective lessors. In June 2020, Flybe Aviation Services was sold to AAG Defence Services Ltd. The Training Academy in Exeter was sold to Devon County Council.

Several parties expressed an interest in purchasing the business and, in October 2020, the Administrators entered into discussions that eventually led to an exchange of contracts for the sale of Flybe, including certain assets, to Thyme Opco Ltd. This new company was established by Cyrus Capital, a former shareholder of Connect Airways. Thyme Opco was to purchase the Flybe brand and relaunch the airline, subject to regulatory approval. The proposed transaction comprised the sale of the Flybe business, company name, brand, some stock and equipment and the transfer of take-off and landing slots at various airports in the UK and Europe. In December 2020, Thyme Opco applied to the CAA for an Operating Licence and Air Operators' Certificate, despite still having the possibility of reactivating the Flybe certificates. The new company also acquired a 21-year old Bombardier Dash 8-Q400 aircraft from Austrian Airlines, registered as G-CLXC, on 20 January 2021.

In preparation for the sale, Flybe was renamed FBE Realisations 2021 Ltd on 6 April 2021. The sale of the business and some assets was completed on 13 April, with the purchaser, Thyme Opco, renamed Flybe Ltd and referred to as Flybe 2.0.

In March 2021, before completion of the sale, the CAA revoked the former Flybe's Operating Licence, despite a further appeal by the Administrators against the decision. On this occasion, the Secretary of State upheld the decision by the CAA in June 2021. The original Operating Licence included 12 pairs (take-off and landing) of valuable legacy slots at Heathrow Airport, worth approximately £10 million. The CAA decided to revoke the Operating Licence on the basis that Flybe 2.0 had no intention of operating the slots and might sell them to generate income. The Heathrow slots were appropriated by British Airways after Flybe went into administration but would have to be returned to Flybe 2.0 if it restarted using the original Operating Licence. Under the circumstances, the slots were returned to the slot co-ordinator, Airport Coordination Ltd.

Flybe 2.0 obtained a new Operating Licence, Air Operators Certificate and route licences in April 2021, enabling it to operate both charter and scheduled passenger services. The new airline leased some 'remedy' slots from British Airways for services from Heathrow to Aberdeen (18 weekly slots) and Edinburgh (25 weekly slots) during the summer season and through to the end of October 2021. British Airways was required to provide the so-called 'remedy' slots to any competitor beginning services on certain routes from Heathrow as part of an agreement with the European Commission following its takeover of British Midland International in 2012, in order to prevent British Airways from dominating the market. In addition, Flybe 2.0 was allocated slots at Birmingham and Manchester, as well obtaining some slots from the former Flybe as part of the sale transaction.

Despite the required licences and slots being in place, Flybe 2.0 did not restart during the summer of 2021 as originally planned, owing to ongoing Covid-19-related travel restrictions and the fact that air travel in the UK was continuing to suffer from a significantly reduced demand. UK domestic flights declined by almost 60 percent during 2021 compared with pre-Covid-19 levels. Also Flybe 2.0 needed time to acquire aircraft and appoint and train flight and cabin crew and support staff. The Dash 8-Q400 (G-CLXC) acquired by Thyme Opco never entered service and left Flybe 2.0 in September 2021.

In late October 2021, Flybe 2.0 appointed David Pflieger as Chief Executive, who brought with him experience of senior management at both Delta Airlines and Virgin America. The airline announced its selection of Birmingham Airport for a new headquarters and primary base, with operations scheduled to begin in early 2022 to key regions across the UK and Europe. The company's marketing slogan was 'Smile and go the extra mile'. A Dash 8-Q400 aircraft, registered as G-JECX, appeared in November 2021 painted in a new white and purple livery.

Ticket sales for Flybe 2.0 opened up in late March 2022, when Belfast City Airport was named as its second base. In total, 23 routes, involving up to 530 flights per week, were offered during the summer of 2022 to serve 16 airports in the UK, France and the Netherlands, with no competition from another airline on at least eight of the routes. A phased introduction of the routes began with Birmingham to Belfast City on 13 April 2022. Six more routes started during April (Belfast–Glasgow, Belfast–Leeds/Bradford, Belfast–Heathrow, Birmingham–Amsterdam, East Midlands–Amsterdam, Leeds Bradford–Heathrow) and three more in May and June (Belfast–Edinburgh, Belfast–Amsterdam, Heathrow–Amsterdam). In July/August 2022, 13 more sectors were due to be added (Belfast–East Midlands, Belfast–Southampton, Belfast–Inverness, Belfast–Manchester, Belfast–Newcastle, Birmingham–Avignon, Birmingham–Brest, Birmingham–Edinburgh, Birmingham–Glasgow, Southampton–Avignon, Southampton–Toulon Hyères, Aberdeen–Birmingham, Aberdeen–Belfast).

Flybe 2.0 began with a fleet of four leased Dash 8-Q400s (G-JECX, G-JECY, G-ECOE and G-ECOR), with plans to increase operations to eight, and ultimately 32 aircraft. More than 600 jobs were created in the new business, including the employment of flight and cabin crew from the former Flybe.

Bombardier (de Havilland) Dash 8-Q402 G-JECX painted in the Flybe 2.0 purple and white livery, during proving flights in December 2021. (Don Bennett)

Two more Dash 8-Q400s were added during summer 2022 (G-FLBA, G-EXTB). However, delays in the delivery of additional aircraft led to the airline reducing the frequency of flights on some of its routes and prevented the introduction of some flights to new destinations. Some of the capacity problems were overcome by leasing an ATR 72-500 from Swiftair and an Embraer E175 from Marathon Airlines.

Flybe's winter schedule 2022/23 is due to include new, additional routes and frequencies from London Heathrow to Newquay, Belfast City to Edinburgh, Birmingham to Glasgow, Edinburgh and Aberdeen, and Southampton to Edinburgh, Glasgow and Manchester. However, the Heathrow to Leeds/Bradford service was withdrawn at the end of October 2022 due to low passenger numbers.

Right: Preparation of Bombardier (de Havilland) Dash 8-Q402 G-JECX for the inaugural flight (BE404) of Flybe 2.0 from Birmingham to Belfast City Airport on 13 April 2022. (James Pearson)

Below: Boarding the inaugural flight from Birmingham to Belfast City. (James Pearson)

The cockpit of Bombardier (de Havilland) Dash 8-Q402 G-JECX. (Rhys Jones)

The 2-2 seating configuration on the Bombardier (de Havilland) Dash 8-Q402 operated by Flybe 2.0. (Rhys Jones)

Newly upholstered seats in blue and purple leather on the Bombardier (de Havilland) Dash 8-Q402. (Rhys Jones)

Right: A commemorative mug to celebrate the launch of flights by Flybe 2.0. (James Pearson)

Below: Bombardier (de Havilland) Dash 8-Q402 G-JECY at Amsterdam in May 2022. (Gerard Helmer)

Bombardier (de Havilland) Dash 8-Q402 G-ECOE is about to land at Glasgow Airport in May 2022. (John Murdoch)

Bombardier (de Havilland) Dash 8-Q402 G-FLBA joined the Flybe 2.0 fleet in July 2022. (John Visanich)

Bombardier (de Havilland) Dash 8-Q402 G-ECOR on final approach to London Heathrow in July 2022. (Fred Willemsen)

Bombardier (de Havilland) Dash 8-Q402 G-EXTB, still to be painted in the full Flybe 2.0 livery, in October 2022. (Dave Richardson)

ATR 72-500 EC-KKQ operated for Flybe 2.0, on lease from Swiftair, during summer 2022. (Don Bennett)

Embraer E175 SX-ASK was wet-leased by Flybe 2.0 from Marathon Airlines from June to September 2022. It is shown at Glasgow in August 2022. (Martin Bridges)

Fleet Lists

Abbreviation used: C/No. = Construction Number; lsd = leased; opby = operated by; opf = operated for; rtl = return to lessor; std = stored; wfu = withdrawn from use.

Sources

airfleets.net
planelogger.com
planespotters.net
twinotterarchive.com
vickersviscount.net

Intra Airways

Aircraft type	C/No.	Registration	Date	Notes/Fate
Britten-Norman BN-2A Islander	180	G-BAVT	May 1973–May 1975	To Brymon Airways
	389	G-BBZD	May 1974–Dec 1974	rtl
Douglas DC-3 Dakota	9043	G-AKNB	Feb 1969–Oct 1978	To Clyden Airways
	13468	G-AMHJ	May 1975–Oct 1979	To EAS
	33185	G-AMPO	Aug 1975–Jul 1978	To Eastern Airways
	26569	G-AMPY	Dec 1970–Oct 1979	To EAS
	32872	G-AMPZ	Mar 1973–Sep 1978	To Clyden Airways
	26735	G-AMRA	Aug 1976–Jul 1978	To Eastern Airways
	32716	G-AMYJ	Aug 1972–Nov 1978	To Eastern Airways
Piper PA23 Aztec	27-2451	G-ASNA	Nov 1972–Feb 1975	opby International Air Charter; To Glamair
Piper PA-23 Apache 235	27-556	G-ASFF	Nov 1972–Feb 1975	opby International Air Charter; To Glamair
Piper PA-31 Navajo	31P-39	G-BFAM	Sep1977–Oct 1979	To Jersey European
Vickers Viscount - 700	14	G-ARGR	Mar 1976–Jun 1976	To Alidair
	52	G-BDRC	Mar 1976–Oct 1977	To Alidair
Vickers Viscount - 800	341	G-BAPE	Oct 1977–Oct 1979	To Jersey European
	344	G-BAPG	Jan 1978–Nov 1978; Feb 1979–Jul 1979; Sep 1979	lsd to Arkia
	375	G-AVJB	Dec 1976–Oct 1979	To EAS

Express Air Freight/Express Air Services (EAF/EAS)

Aircraft type	C/No.	Registration	Date	Notes/Fate
Douglas DC-3 Dakota	9043	G-AKNB	Jan 1977–Oct 1978	opby Intra; To Clyden Airways
	32872	G-AMPZ	Jan 1977–Sep 1978	opby Intra; To Clyden Airways
	13468	G-AMHJ	Nov 1979–Feb 1982	To Air Atlantique
	26569	G-AMPY	Nov 1979–Feb 1982	To Air Atlantique
Handley Page HPR.7 Dart Herald Series 200	189	G-ATDS	Aug 1977–Nov 1984	To Channel Express
	174	G-BEZB	Aug 1977–Nov 1984	To Channel Express
	195	G-BFRJ	Apr 1978–Mar 1984	To Aligiulia
	197	G-BFRK	Apr 1978–Jan 1985	To Aligiulia
Vickers Viscount 800	341	G-BAPE	Mar 1980–Apr 1980; Oct 1980	To Southern International
	344	G-BAPG	Jan 1981	To Southern International

Jersey European Airways

Aircraft type	C/No.	Registration	Date	Notes/Fate
BAC 1-11 510ED	BAC.139	G-AVMK	Mar 1997–Oct 1998	rtl
Canadair (Bombardier) CRJ200ER	7345	G-JECA	Oct 1999–Jun 2000	To British European
British Aerospace 146-100	E1010	G-JEAO	Sep 1994–Jun 2000	opf Air France (Oct 1996–Jun 2000); To British European
	E1071	G-JEAT	Oct 1996–Jun 2000	opf Air France (Oct 1996–Jun 2000; To British European
	E1035	G-JEAU	Dec 1996–Jun 2000	opf Air France (Sep 1999–Jun 2000); To British European
	E1003	EI-CPY	Oct 1999–Jun 2000	opby Cityjet; To British European
British Aerospace 146-200	E2060	D-AZUR	Oct 1996–Mar 1997	lsd from Hamburg Airlines
	E2099	G-OLCA	Mar 1993–Sep 1993	Re-registered as G-JEAJ
	E2099	G-JEAJ	Sep 1993–Jun 2000	To British European
	E2103	G-JEAK	Mar 1993–Jun 2000	lsd to Cityjet Mar–Sep 2000; To British European
	E2018	G-JEAR	Nov 1995–Jun 2000	opf Air France (Feb 1998–Jun 2000); To British European
	E2020	G-JEAS	Feb 1996–Jun 2000	opf Air France (Aug 1997–Jun 2000); To British European
	E2064	G-JEAV	Jun 1997–Jun 2000	To British European
	E2059	G-JEAW	Jul 1997–Jun 2000	To British European
	E2136	G-JEAX	Feb 1998–Jun 2000	To British European

Aircraft type	C/No.	Registration	Date	Notes/Fate
British Aerospace 146-300	E3129	G-JEAL	Apr 1993–Dec 1998	opf Air France (Dec 1997–Dec 1999); To Aer Lingus
	E3128	G-JEAM	May 1993–Dec 1998; Mar 2000–Jun 2000	lsd to BRA/BA (Dec 1998–Sep 1999); lsd to Cityjet (Sep 1999–Mar 2000); To British European
	E3181	G-JEBA	Jun 1998–Jun 2000	opf Air France (Jun 1998–Jun 2000); To British European
	E3185	G-JEBB	Jun 1998–Jun 2000	opf Air France (Jun 1998–Jun 2000); To British European
	E3189	G-JEBC	Jun 1998–Jun 2000	To British European
	E3191	G-JEBD	Jul 1998–Jun 2000	To British European
	E3206	G-JEBE	May 1998–Jun 2000	To British European
Britten-Norman BN-2A-26 Islander	2004	G-BESO	Jan 1980–Jun 1983	To Air Orkney
	496	G-BDNP	Jan 1980–Sep 1981	Written-off after crash at Guernsey
	150	G-AXXJ	Mar 1983–Oct 1984	To Air Wright
de Havilland DHC-6-310 Twin Otter	347	VP-FAQ	Apr 1981–Apr 1982	lsd from British Antarctic Survey; Re-registered as G-BKBC
	347	G-BKBC	Apr 1982–Feb 1986	To NFK Orkney
	546	VP-FAW	Jul 1981–Sep 1981	lsd from British Antarctic Survey
	783	VP-FBB	Jul 1982–Aug 1982	lsd from British Antarctic Survey
	787	VP-FBC	May 1982–Sep 1982	lsd from British Antarctic Survey
	571	G-BFGP	Oct 1985–May 1986	rtl
	629	G-BGMD	Nov 1983–Aug 1985; Feb 1989–Jul 1989	To BAC Charter
	682	G-BGZP	Nov 1983–Jun1985; Sep1988–Apr 1989	To BAC Charter
	513	G-BLIS	Apr 1980–Jun 1980; Jul 1980–Aug 1980	To Scibe Airlift Société Commerciale et Industrielle Bemba
	617	G-BGMC	Nov 1983–Oct 1985; Oct 1987–Jan 1988	Re-registered as G-JEAC
	617	G-JEAC	Mar 1988–Apr 1989	To Guide Leasing
	699	G-OJEA	Jul 1980–Feb 1985	To RRC Air Services
Bombardier (de Havilland) DHC-8-Q201	541	G-JEDX	Feb–Jun 2000	To British European
	542	G-JEDY	Mar–Jun 2000	To British European
	547	G-JEDZ	Jun 2000	To British European

Aircraft type	C/No.	Registration	Date	Notes/Fate
Bombardier (de Havilland) DHC-8-Q311	309	G-JEDA	Jun 1999–Jun 2000	To British European
	323	G-JEDB	Jul 1999–Jun 2000	To British European
	532	G-JEDC	Oct 1999–Jun 2000	To British European
	533	G-JEDD	Oct 1999–Jun 2000	To British European
	534	G-JEDE	Nov 1999–Jun 2000	To British European
Embraer EMB-110 Bandeirante	110270	G-BHJZ	May 1980–Sep 1992	To Willow Air
	110234	G-BGYT	Oct 1985–Dec 1986	To Euroair
	110249	G-BGYV	Oct 1985–Feb1988	To Business Air
	110256	G-BHJY	Mar1980–Jan 1982	To Euroair
	110288	G-BIBE	Nov 1985–Oct 1987	To Travelair
Fokker F27-100	10228	G-RNSY	Dec 1983–Mar 1984	To Mesaba Airlines
Fokker F27-200	10225	G-BAUR	May 1995–Dec 1995	Scrapped
Fokker F27-500	10627	G-JEAD	Oct 1990–Aug 1997	To BAC Express
	10633	G-JEAE	Jan1991–Jan 1994; May 1994–Oct 1999	To Channel Express
	10637	G-JEAF	Dec 1990–Sep 1994; Aug 1996–Aug 1999	To Eureca
	10639	G-JEAG	Nov 1990–Jun 1994; Oct 1995–Oct 1999	To Sky Team
	10664	G-JEAA	Mar1988–Jul 1995	To UP Air
	10667	G-JEAB	Apr 1988–Oct 1993; Nov 1994–Mar 1995	To UP Air
	10669	VH-EWY	Oct 1990–Jan 1991	Re-registered as G-JEAH
	10669	G-JEAH	Jan 1991–Dec 1999	To BAC Express
	10672	VH-EWZ	Aug 1990–Dec 1990	Re-registered as G-JEAI
	10672	G-JEAI	Dec 1990–Apr 2000	To Euroceltic Airways
Hawker Siddeley 748-2A	1677	G-BPNK	Mar 1989–Jun1989	To Kel Air
	1766	G-BGMN	Dec 1989–Jul 1992	To Airfast Indonesia
	1767	G-BGMO	Oct 1989–Oct 1991	To Euroair
	1714	G-BMFT	Apr 1990–Oct 1991	To Emerald Airlines
Piper PA-31 Navajo	31P-39	G-BFAM	Nov 1979–Apr 1982	
Short SD330	3006	G-BEEO	Feb 1984–Jun 1987	To British Air Ferries
	3077	G-BJFK	Apr 1985–Oct 1987	To National Airways
	3082	G-BJUK	Jun 1985–Apr 1988	To Gill Airways
Short SD360	3603	G-OJSY	Mar 1986–May 1992	To Business Air
	3608	G-BKMX	Oct 1998–Jun 2000	To BAC Express
	3661	G-BLRT	Dec 1986–Aug 1987	To Connectair
	3676	G-BLZT	Mar 1992–Dec 1994	To Gill Airways
	3712	G-OBLK	Jan 1987–Feb 1990; Apr 1991–Jun 2000	To British European
	3713	G-OBOH	Jan 1987–May 1996	To BAC Express
	3714	G-OBHD	Mar 1987–Mar 1990; May 1991–Jun 2000	To British European
	3736	G-VBAC	Sep 1997–Apr 1998	To BAC Express

Aircraft type	C/No.	Registration	Date	Notes/Fate
Vickers Viscount-814	341	G-BAPE	Nov 1979–Dec 1979	lsd to Arkia then to EAS
	344	G-BAPG	Dec 1979–Mar 1980	lsd to British Midland then to EAS
	375	G-AVJB	Apr 1980–Nov 1980	To Field Aviation

British European

Aircraft type	C/No.	Registration	Date	Notes/Fate
Canadair (Bombardier) CRJ200ER	7345	G-JECA	Jun 2000–Jul 2002	opf Air France; To Flybe
	7393	G-JECB	Jun 2000–Jul 2002	To Flybe
	7434	G-JECC	Oct 2000–Jul 2002	To Flybe
	7469	G-JECD	Jan 2001–Jul 2002	opf Air France; To Flybe
British Aerospace 146-100	E1010	G-JEAO	Jun 2000–Mar 2002	opf Air France (Jun 2000–Mar 2002); To BAe Systems
	E1071	G-JEAT	Jun 2000–Jul 2002	opf Air France (Jun 2000–Jul 2002); To Flybe
	E1035	G-JEAU	Jun 2000–Jul 2002	opf Air France (Jun 2000–Jul 2002); To Flybe
	E1003	EI-CPY	Jun 2000–Oct 2000	opby Cityjet
British Aerospace 146-200	E2018	G-JEAR	Jun 2000–Jul 2002	opf Air France (Jun 2000–Jul 2002); To Flybe
	E2020	G-JEAS	Jun 2000–Jul 2002	To Flybe
	E2059	G-JEAW	Jun 2000–Jul 2002	To Flybe
	E2064	G-JEAV	Jun 2000–Jul 2002	To Flybe
	E2099	G-JEAJ	Jun 2000–Jul 2002	To Flybe
	E2103	G-JEAK	Oct 2000–Jul 2002	To Flybe
	E2136	G-JEAX	Jun 2000–Jul 2002	To Flybe
	E2138	G-JEAY	Mar 2001–Jul 2002	To Flybe
British Aerospace 146-300	E3128	G-JEAM	Jun 2000–Jul 2002	To Flybe
	E3181	G-JEBA	Jun 2000–Jul 2002	opf Air France (Jun 2000–Jul 2002); To Flybe
	E3185	G-JEBB	Jun 2000–Jul 2002	opf Air France (Jun 2000–Jul 2002); To Flybe
	E3189	G-JEBC	Jun 2000–Jul 2002	To Flybe
	E3191	G-JEBD	Jun 2000–Jul 2002	To Flybe
	E3206	G-JEBE	Jun 2000–Jul 2002	To Flybe
Bombardier (de Havilland) DHC-8-Q201	541	G-JEDX	Jun 2000–Jul 2002	To Flybe
	542	G-JEDY	Jun 2000–Jul 2002	To Flybe
	547	G-JEDZ	Jun 2000–Jul 2002	To Flybe
Bombardier (de Havilland) DHC-8-Q311	309	G-JEDA	Jun 2000–Apr 2002	rtl
	323	G-JEDB	Jun 2000–Jul 2002	To Flybe
	532	G-JEDC	Jun 2000–Jul 2002	To Flybe
	533	G-JEDD	Jun 2000–Jul 2002	To Flybe
	534	G-JEDE	Jun 2000–Jul 2002	To Flybe
	548	G-JEDF	Jul 2000–Jul 2002	To Flybe

Aircraft type	C/No.	Registration	Date	Notes/Fate
Bombardier (de Havilland) DHC-8-Q402	4052	G-JEDI	Oct 2001–Jul 2002	To Flybe
	4058	G-JEDJ	Jan–Jul 2002	To Flybe
	3712	G-OBLK	Jun–Oct 2000	To BAC Express
Shorts 360	3714	G-OBHD	Jun 2000–Nov 2001	To Emerald Airways

Flybe

Aircraft type	C/No.	Registration	Date	Notes/Fate
ATR 42-500	546	G-ISLF	Jun 2016–Nov 2018	opby Blue Islands; To Elix Aviation
ATR 72-500	748	EI-REL	Jun 2014–Mar 2019	opby Stobart Air; To Stobart Air
	760	EI-REM	Jul 2014–Apr 2019	opby Stobart Air; To Stobart Air
	529	G-ISLI	May 2017–Mar 2019	opby Blue Islands; rtl
	634	G-ISLK	Oct 2016–Mar 2020	opby Blue Islands
	696	G-ISLL	Jan 2017–Mar 2020	opby Blue Islands
ATR 72-600	1295	EI-FMJ	Sep 2017–Mar 2020	opby Stobart Air; To Stobart Air
	1260	G-FBXA	Sep 2015–Feb 2020	opf SAS (Sep 2015–Oct 2019); To Loganair
	1277	G-FBXB	Oct 2015–Feb 2020	opf SAS (Oct 2015–Dec 2019); To Loganair
	1300	G-FBXC	Dec 2015–Jan 2020	opf SAS (Dec 2015–Dec 2019); To Stobart Air
	1315	G-FBXD	Mar 2016–Feb 2020	opf SAS (Mar 2016–Jan 2020); To Stobart Air
	1322	G-FBXE	Apr 2016–Oct 2019	opf SAS (Apr 2016–Feb 2019); To Stobart Air
Boeing 737-300	24059	G-STRA	Dec 2005–Nov 2006	To Astraeus
	24255	G-STRB	May 2005–Dec 2005	To Astraeus
	28572	G-STRE	Mar 2005–Nov 2006	To Astraeus
	25011	G-STRI	May 2005–Dec 2006	To Astraeus
Canadair (Bombardier) CRJ200ER	7345	G-JECA	Jul 2002–Nov 2003	opf Air France; To Air Sahara
	7393	G-JECB	Jul 2002–Oct 2003	To Air Sahara
	7434	G-JECC	Jul 2002–Jul 2003	To Air Sahara
	7469	G-JECD	Jul 2002–Sep 2003	opf Air France; To Air Sahara
British Aerospace 146-100	E1071	G-JEAT	Jul 2002–Apr 2003	opf Air France Express (Jul 2002–Apr 2003); wfu
	E1035	G-JEAU	Jul 2002–Dec 2003	opf Air France (Jul 2002–Dec 2003);wfu
	E1015	G-MABR	Mar–Jul 2007	To Trygon Aviation
British Aerospace 146-200	E2018	G-JEAR	Jul 2002–Jan 2003	opf Air France (Jul 2002–Jan 2003); To BAe Systems
	E2020	G-JEAS	Jul 2002–Oct 2007	opf Air France (Nov 2002–Dec 2004); wfu

Aircraft type	C/No.	Registration	Date	Notes/Fate
	E2036	G-GNTZ	Mar 2007–Jun 2008	wfu
	E2059	G-JEAW	Jul 2002–Jan 2007	rtl
	E2064	G-JEAV	Jul 2002–Nov 2006	rtl
	E2088	G-MANS	Mar 2007–Dec 2007	wfu
	E2099	G-JEAJ	Jul 2002–Mar 2007	rtl
	E2103	G-JEAK	Jul 2002–Mar 2007	rtl
	E2136	G-JEAX	Jul 2002–Jan 2006	To Cityjet
	E2138	G-JEAY	Jul 2002–Jan 2007	rtl
British Aerospace 146-300	E3123	G-UKHP	Jun 2003–Jan 2004	To Cityjet
	E3128	G-JEAM	Jul 2002–Apr 2008	wfu
	E3171	G-OINV	Mar 2007–Jan 2008	wfu
	E3181	G-JEBA	Jul 2002–Oct 2008	opf Air France (Jul 2002–Apr 2005); To Star Peru
	E3185	G-JEBB	Jul 2002–Nov 2007	opf Air France (Jul 2002–Apr 2005); To Star Peru
	E3189	G-JEBC	Jul 2002–Oct 2007	To Aviastar
	E3191	G-JEBD	Jul 2002–Mar 2008	To Air Libya
	E3202	G-BTUY	Jul 2003–Jun 2004	Re-registered G-JEBF
	E3202	G-JEBF	Jun 2004–Jun 2008	To Bank of Scotland
	E3205	G-JEBH	Dec 2003–Nov 2004	To Flightline
	E3206	G-JEBE	Jul 2002–May 2008	To Astra Airlines
	E3209	G-BVCE	Jul 2003–Jul 2004	Re-registered G-JEBG
	E3209	G-JEBG	Jul 2004–Jun 2008	To Bank of Scotland
British Aerospace Jetstream 41	41032	G-MAJA	N/A	opby Eastern Airways
	41070	G-MAJK	Sep 2017–Feb 2019	opby Eastern Airways
	41087	G-MAJL	N/A	opby Eastern Airways
	41099	G-MAJY	N/A	opby Eastern Airways
	41100	G-MAJZ	N/A	opby Eastern Airways
De Havilland DHC-6-310 Twin Otter	666	G-BVVK	Mar 2009–Sep 2017	opby Loganair
	696	G-BZFP	Mar 2009–Jul 2015	opby Loganair; To RUAG Holding
Bombardier (de Havilland) DHC-8-Q201	541	G-JEDX	Jul 2002–Apr 2004	rtl
	542	G-JEDY	Jul 2002–Apr 2004	rtl
	547	G-JEDZ	Jul 2002–Apr 2004	rtl
Bombardier (de Havilland) DHC-8-Q311	323	G-JEDB	Jul–Sep 2002	rtl
	451	G-NVSA	Mar–Sep 2007	To CHC Global Operations Canada
	458	G-BRYU	Mar–Jul 2007	To Medavia
	462	G-BRYV	Mar–Jun 2007	To Air Tanzania
	464	G-BRYZ	Mar–May 2007	To GMG Airlines
	474	G-BRYW	Mar–Jul 2007	To Air Tanzania
	519	G-BRYY	Mar–May 2007	To Air Panama
	532	G-JEDC	Jul 2002–Mar 2004	rtl
	533	G-JEDD	Jul 2002–Jun 2004	rtl

Aircraft type	C/No.	Registration	Date	Notes/Fate
	534	G-JEDE	Jul 2002–Apr 2004	rtl
	548	G-JEDF	Jul 2002–Mar 2005	rtl
Bombardier (de Havilland) DHC-8-Q402	4052	G-JEDI	Jul 2002–Dec 2013	To DAC Aviation International
	4058	G-JEDJ	Jul 2002–Aug 2012	rtl
	4065	G-JEDK	Apr 2002–Apr 2012	rtl
	4067	G-JEDL	Jun 2002–May 2012	rtl
	4077	G-JEDM	Jul 2003–Jan 2020	rtl
	4078	G-JEDN	Jul 2003–May 2013	To Aero Contractors
	4079	G-JEDO	Jul 2003–Jan 2013	To Aero Contractors
	4085	G-JEDP	Jan 2004–Mar 2020	rtl
	4087	G-JEDR	Mar 2004–Feb 2020	rtl
	4088	G-JEDT	Mar 2004–Mar 2020	rtl
	4089	G-JEDU	Apr 2004–Mar 2020	rtl
	4090	G-JEDV	May 2004–Mar 2020	rtl
	4093	G-JEDW	Jul 2004–Mar 2020	rtl
	4094	G-JECE	Aug 2004–Jun 2017	rtl
	4095	G-JECF	Oct 2004–Aug 2017	rtl
	4098	G-JECG	Jan 2005–Sep 2017	rtl
	4103	G-JECH	Apr 2005–May 2017	rtl
	4105	G-JECI	Jun 2005–Oct 2017	rtl
	4110	G-JECJ	Dec 2005–Nov 2017	rtl
	4113	G-JECK	Jan 2006–Mar 2020	rtl
	4114	G-JECL	Jan 2006–Mar 2020	rtl
	4118	G-JECM	Apr 2006–Mar 2020	rtl
	4120	G-JECN	Apr 2006–Mar 2020	rtl
	4126	G-JECO	Jul 2006–Mar 2020	rtl
	4136	G-JECP	Oct 2006–Mar 2020	rtl
	4139	G-JECR	Dec 2006–Mar 2020	rtl
	4142	G-JECS	Jan 2007–Jul 2011	To South African Express Airways
	4144	G-JECT	Jan 2007–Jul 2011	To South African Express Airways
	4146	G-JECU	Feb 2007–Jul 2011	To South African Express Airways
	4148	G-JECV	Apr 2007–Sep 2009	To Olympic Air
	4152	G-JECW	Apr 2007–Sep 2009	To Olympic Air
	4155	G-JECX	Jun 2007–Mar 2020	rtl
	4157	G-JECY	Jun 2007–Mar 2020	opf Brussels Airlines (Sep 2012–Mar 2014); rtl
	4179	G-JECZ	Nov 2007–Mar 2020	rtl
	4180	G-ECOA	Dec 2007–Feb 2020	rtl
	4185	G-ECOB	Jan 2008–Mar 2020	lsd to Wideroe (Aug 2008–Jun 2009); rtl
	4187	G-PRPA	May 2015–Mar 2020	rtl

Aircraft type	C/No.	Registration	Date	Notes/Fate
	4188	G-PRPM	Apr 2017–Mar 2020	rtl
	4191	G-PRPG	Nov 2016–Mar 2020	rtl
	4195	G-PRPF	Dec 2016–Mar 2020	rtl
	4197	G-ECOC	Mar 2008–Mar 2020	lsd to Wideroe (Nov 2008–Dec 2009); rtl
	4201	G-KKEV	Apr 2008–Mar 2020	rtl
	4202	G-PRPJ	Dec 2016–Mar 2020	rtl
	4203	G-PRPK	Feb 2017–Mar 2020	rtl
	4204	G-PRPI	Sep 2016–Mar 2020	rtl
	4206	G-ECOD	Jul 2008–Mar 2020	rtl
	4209	G-PRPE	Apr 2016–Mar 2020	rtl
	4212	G-ECOE	Jul 2008–Mar 2020	lsd to Wideroe (Oct 2008–Jul 2009); lsd to Olympic Air (Aug 2009–Jun 2010) ; rtl
	4213	G-PRPN	Mar 2017–Mar 2020	rtl
	4214	G-PRPO	May 2017–Mar 2020	rtl
	4216	G-ECOF	Aug 2008–Mar 2020	lsd to Wideroe (Sep 2008–Sep 2009); lsd to Olympic Air (Sep 2009–Aug 2010) ; rtl
	4220	G-ECOG	Oct 2008–Mar 2020	rtl
	4221	G-ECOH	Oct 2008–Mar 2020	opf Brussels Airlines (Mar 2012–May 2014); rtl
	4224	G-ECOI	Nov 2008–Mar 2020	opf Brussels Airlines (Mar 2012–Oct 2017); rtl
	4229	G-ECOJ	Jan 2009–Mar 2020	rtl
	4230	G-ECOK	Jan 2009–Mar 2020	opf Brussels Airlines (Oct 2012–Oct 2017); rtl
	4233	G-ECOM	Dec 2008–Mar 2020	rtl
	4237	G-ECOO	Jan 2009–Feb 2020	rtl
	4242	G-ECOP	Apr 2009–Mar 2020	rtl
	4258	G-ECOR	Apr 2009–Mar 2020	rtl
	4251	G-ECOT	May 2009–Mar 2020	rtl
	4021	G-ECOW	Aug 2008–Jul 2010	To Bombardier
	4022	G-ECOY	Sep 2008–Aug 2010	rtl
	4022	G-ECOV	Jul 2008–Feb 2011	rtl
	4034	G-ECOZ	Oct 2008–Feb 2011	rtl
	4253	G-FLBA	Jul 2009–Mar 2020	rtl
	4255	G-FLBB	Jul 2009–Feb 2020	rtl
	4257	G-FLBC	Jul 2009–Mar 2020	rtl
	4259	G-FLBD	Jul 2009–Mar 2020	lsd to Olympic Air (Aug 2009-Oct 2010); rtl
	4261	G-FLBE	Oct 2009–Mar 2020	lsd to Olympic Air (Oct 2009-Oct 2010); rtl
	4323	G-PRPH	Oct 2016–Mar 2020	rtl

Aircraft type	C/No.	Registration	Date	Notes/Fate
	4332	G-PRPD	Nov 2015–Mar 2020	rtl
	4333	G-PRPB	Jul 2015–Mar 2020	rtl
	4338	G-PRPC	Aug 2015–Mar 2020	rtl
	4344	G-FLBF	Jan–Oct 2011	To South African Express Airways
	4350	G-FLBG	Apr–Aug 2011	To South African Express Airways
	4366	G-FLBH	Jun–Sep 2011	To South African Express Airways
	4370	G-FLBJ	Jul–Sep 2011	To South African Express Airways
	4380	G-PRPL	Apr 2015–Mar 2020	rtl
Dornier DO-328	3022	G-BWWT	Feb 2012–Feb 2016	opby Suckling Airways/ Loganair; To MHS Aviation
	3062	G-BYMK	Mar 2014–Jul 2017	opby Loganair; wfu
	3101	G-CCGS	Apr 2015–Jul 2017	opby Loganair;
Embraer ERJ145	145024	G-EMBC	Mar–Oct 2007	To Port One Ltd
	145039	G-EMBD	Mar–Nov 2007	To Dniproavia
	145042	G-EMBE	Mar–Oct 2007	To Dniproavia
	145088	G-EMBF	Mar–Aug 2007	To Dniproavia
	145094	G-EMBG	Mar–Aug 2007	To Dniproavia
	145107	G-EMBH	Mar 2007–Sep 2008	To Athens Airways
	145126	G-EMBI	Mar 2007–Mar 2009	To bmi Regional
	145134	G-EMBJ	Mar 2007–Apr 2009	To bmi Regional
	145167	G-EMBK	Mar 2007–Nov 2008	To Aircraft Solutions
	145177	G-EMBL	Mar 2007–Mar 2009	To Aircraft Solutions
	145196	G-EMBM	Mar 2007–Mar 2009	To Aircraft Solutions
	145201	G-EMBN	Mar 2007–Jun 2008	To bmi Regional
	145219	G-EMBO	Mar 2007–Aug 2008	To Andalus Lineas Aereas
	145229	G-ERJA	Mar 2007–May 2009	To FALAK Aviation
	145237	G-ERJB	Mar 2007–Oct 2008	To Dniproavia
	145253	G-ERJC	Mar 2007–May 2009	To FALAK Aviation
	145290	G-ERJD	Mar 2007–Nov 2008	To Dniproavia
	145300	G-EMBP	Mar 2007–Sep 2008	To Aircraft Solutions
	145315	G-ERJE	Mar 2007–Oct 2008	To Dniproavia
	145325	G-ERJF	Mar 2007–Jul 2008	To Dniproavia
	145357	G-EMBS	Mar–Dec 2007	To Dniproavia
	145394	G-ERJG	Mar 2007–Apr 2008	To Dniproavia
	145404	G-EMBT	Mar–Nov 2007	To Dniproavia
	145458	G-EMBU	Mar 2007–Dec 2008	To Aircraft Solutions
	145482	G-EMBV	Mar 2007–Jan 2009	To Aircraft Solutions
	145546	G-EMBW	Mar 2007–Mar 2009	To Aircraft Solutions
	145573	G-EMBX	Mar 2007–Jan 2009	To Aircraft Solutions
	145617	G-EMBY	Mar 2007–Feb 2009	To Aircraft Solutions
	145405	G-CHMR	N/A	opby Eastern Airways

Aircraft type	C/No.	Registration	Date	Notes/Fate
Embraer E170-100	17000111	G-CIXV	Sep 2017–Oct 2018	opby Eastern Airways
Embraer E175-200	17000326	G-FBJA	Nov 2011–Mar 2020	To Flybe Leasing
	17000327	G-FBJB	Dec 2011–Mar 2020	To Flybe Leasing
	17000328	G-FBJC	Nov 2011–Mar 2020	To Flybe Leasing
	17000329	G-FBJD	Dec 2011–Mar 2020	To Flybe Leasing
	17000336	G-FBJE	Apr 2012–Mar 2020	To Flybe Leasing
	17000341	G-FBJF	May 2012–Mar 2020	To Flybe Leasing
	17000344	G-FBJG	Jun 2012–Nov 2019	rtl
	17000351	G-FBJH	Sep 2012–Nov 2019	rtl
	17000355	G-FBJI	Nov 2012–Mar 2020	rtl
	17000358	G-FBJJ	Dec 2013–Mar 2020	rtl
	17000359	G-FBJK	Dec 2013–Mar 2020	To CAW Finance Group
Embraer E195-200	19000029	G-FBEA	Sep 2006–Aug 2014	To KalStar Aviation
	19000057	G-FBEB	Dec 2006–Oct 2014	To KalStar Aviation
	19000069	G-FBEC	Mar 2007–Mar 2014	rtl
	19000084	G-FBED	Jun 2007–Mar 2014	rtl
	19000093	G-FBEE	Jul 2007–Apr 2014	rtl
	19000104	G-FBEF	Sep 2007–Aug 2019	wfu/std (Apr 2014-Mar 2015); opf Stobart Air (Nov 2017–Aug 2019); rtl
	19000120	G-FBEG	Nov 2007–Oct 2019	rtl
	19000128	G-FBEH	Nov 2007–Sep 2019	std (Apr 2014–Aug 2014); opf Stobart Air (Nov 2017–Dec 2018); rtl
	19000143	G-FBEI	Jan 2008–Dec 2019	rtl
	19000155	G-FBEJ	Mar 2008–Jan 2020	opf Helvetic Airways (Jul 2014-Aug 2014); rtl
	19000168	G-FBEK	Apr 2008–Feb 2020	wfu/std (Jan 2014–Feb 2016); rtl
	19000184	G-FBEL	Jun 2008–Sep 2018	wfu/std (Jan 2014–Mar 2016); To Stobart Air
	19000204	G-FBEM	Aug 2008–Jul 2018	wfu/std (Apr 2014-Jun 2015); To Stobart Air
	19000213	G-FBEN	Oct 2008–Mar 2018	opf Augigny Air Services (Mar 2014–Jul 2014); wfu/std (Oct 2014–Jun 2015); To Stobart Air
	19000213	EI-GGC	Jun 2018–Feb 2019	opby Stobart Air; To Stobart Air
Saab 340B	340B-160	G-LGNI	Oct 2008–Sep 2017	opby Loganair
	340B-169	G-LGND	Oct 2008–Sep 2017	Opby Loganair
	340B-172	G-LGNE	Oct 2008–Sep 2017	Opby Loganair
	340B-173	G-LGNJ	Oct 2008–Aug 2017	Opby Loganair

Aircraft type	C/No.	Registration	Date	Notes/Fate
	340B-185	G-LGNK	Oct 2008–Jul 2017	Opby Loganair
	340B-187	G-LGNM	Oct 2008–Sep 2016	Opby Loganair
	340B-192	G-LGNF	Oct 2008–Sep 2017	Opby Loganair; To RVL Aviation
	340B-197	G-LGNN	Apr 2008–Feb 2017	Opby Loganair
	340B-199	G-LGNA	Oct 2008–Aug 2017	Opby Loganair
	340B-216	G-LGNB	Oct 2008–Sep 2017	Opby Loganair
	340B-246	G-LGNL	Oct 2008–Jan 2015	wfu
	340B-318	G-LGNC	Oct 2008–Sep 2017	opby Loganair; To NyxAir
	340B-327	G-LGNG	Oct 2008–Aug 2017	Opby Loganair
	340B-333	G-LGNH	Oct 2008–Mar 2017	Opby Loganair
Saab 2000	2000-004	G-LGNR	Nov 2014-Sep 2017	Opby Loganair; to Bank of Utah
	2000-013	G-LGNO	Mar 2014–May 2017	Opby Loganair; To NyxAir

Flybe Finland

Aircraft type	C/No.	Registration	Date	Notes/Fate
ATR 42-500	643	OH-ATB	Oct 2011–Sep 2012	To Solenta Aviation
	651	OH-ATC	Oct 2011–Aug 2014	To Easyfly
	655	OH-ATD	Oct 2011–Aug 2014	To Easyfly
ATR 72-500	741	OH-ATE	Oct 2011–Jun 2015	To Nordic Regional Airlines (NORRA)
	744	OH-ATF	Oct 2011–Jun 2015	To NORRA
	757	OH-ATG	Oct 2011–Jun 2015	To NORRA
	769	OH-ATH	Oct 2011–Jun 2015	To NORRA
	783	OH-ATI	Oct 2011–Jun 2015	To NORRA
	792	OH-ATJ	Oct 2011–Jun 2015	To NORRA
	848	OH-ATK	Oct 2011–May 2015	To NORRA
	851	OH-ATL	Oct 2011–May 2015	To NORRA
	916	OH-ATM	Oct 2011–May 2015	To NORRA
	959	OH-ATN	Oct 2011–May 2015	To NORRA
	977	OH-ATO	Nov 2011–May 2015	To NORRA
	1050	OH-ATP	Oct 2012–May 2015	To NORRA
Embraer E170	17000120	OH-LEI	Oct 2011–Mar 2015	To Finnair
	17000127	OH-LEK	Oct 2011–Mar 2015	rtl
Embraer E190LR	19000059	OH-LKE	Oct 2012–Mar 2015	To Finnair
	19000066	OH-LKF	Oct 2012–Mar 2015	To Finnair
	19000079	OH-LKG	Oct 2012–Mar 2015	To Finnair
	19000086	OH-LKH	Oct 2012–Mar 2015	To Finnair
	19000117	OH-LKI	Oct 2012–Mar 2015	To Finnair
	19000127	OH-LKK	Oct 2012–Mar 2015	To Finnair
	19000153	OH-LKL	Oct 2012–Mar 2015	To Finnair

Aircraft type	C/No.	Registration	Date	Notes/Fate
	19000160	OH-LKM	Oct 2012–Mar 2015	To Finnair
	19000252	OH-LKN	Oct 2012–Mar 2015	To Finnair
	19000267	OH-LKO	Oct 2012–Mar 2015	To Finnair
	19000416	OH-LKP	Oct 2012–Mar 2015	To Finnair
	19000436	OH-LKR	Oct 2012–Mar 2015	To Finnair

Flybe 2.0

Aircraft type	C/No.	Registration	Date	Notes/Fate
ATR 72-500	763	EC-KKQ	Jun 2022–Present	On lease from Swiftair
de Havilland DHC-8-Q402	4155	G-JECX	Nov 2021–Present	
	4157	G-JECY	Feb 2022–Present	
	4212	G-ECOE	Apr 2022–Present	
	4248	G-ECOR	May 2022–Present	Damaged in hard landing (Jun 2022)
	4253	G-FLBA	Jul 2022–Present	
	4411	G-EXTB	Jul 2022–Present	
	4424	G-EXTA	Sep 2022–Present	
	4242	G-ECOP	On order	
	4255	G-FLBB	On order	
	4114	G-JECL	On order	
	4136	G-JECP	On order	
	4093	G-JEDW	On order	
Embraer E175	17000330	SX-ASK	Jun–Sep 2022	On lease from Marathon Airlines

Bibliography

Books
Falconer Jonathan, *Modern Civil Airliners*, JJN Publishing (2021)

Halford-MacLeod Guy, *British Airlines Volume Three: 1964 to Deregulation*, The History Press (2010)

Kelly Cianan, *Connecting the UK: the Story of Britain's Regional Airline*, independently published (2021)

Merton Jones A C, *British Independent Airlines 1946–1976*, The Aviation Hobby Shop (2000)

Wragg David, *The World's Major Airlines* (2nd Edition), Sutton Publishing (2007)

Reports
Various annual reports of the Flybe Group plc, 2008–18

Magazines
Regional Airliners, Airliner World Special, Key Publishing Ltd

Various issues of
Air International, Key Publishing Ltd
Aircraft illustrated, Ian Allen Publishing
Airliner World, Key Publishing Ltd
Aviation News, Key Publishing Ltd
Propliner magazine

Electronic Media
Wickstead Maurice J, *Airlines of the British Isles Since 1919*, Air-Britain (Historians) Ltd (2014)

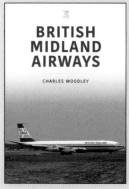
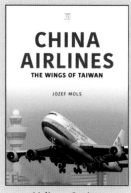
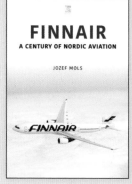